IMMODERATE GREATNESS

Also by William Ophuls
Ecology and the Politics of Scarcity
Requiem for Modern Politics
Plato's Revenge: Politics in the Age of Ecology

IMMODERATE GREATNESS

Why Civilizations Fail

William Ophuls

Copyright © 2012 William Ophuls
All rights reserved.
ISBN: 1479243140
ISBN-13: 9781479243143
Library Congress Control Number: 2012916668
CreateSpace Independent Publishing Platform
North Charleston, South Carolina

The decline of Rome was the natural and inevitable effect of immoderate greatness. Prosperity ripened the principle of decay; the causes of destruction multiplied with the extent of conquest; and as soon as time or accident had removed the artificial supports, the stupendous fabric yielded to the pressure of its own weight.

Edward Gibbon[1]

Contents

Preface   i

Introduction: Immoderate Greatness   1

Biophysical Limits

1. Ecological Exhaustion   7
2. Exponential Growth   13
3. Expedited Entropy   21
4. Excessive Complexity   31

Human Error

5. Moral Decay   45
6. Practical Failure   55

Conclusion: Trampled Down, Barren, and Bare   65

Bibliographic Note   71

Notes   77

Selected Sources   95

Index   105

Preface

This book weaves together many strands of thought to explain why civilizations decline and fall. None of the strands in this short, synoptic overview is original. However, my synthesis of biophysical, moral, and practical factors is, I believe, original and points toward a conclusion that most will find both novel and unpalatable: civilization is effectively hardwired for self-destruction.[1]

To this end, I abstract, from a long and complex historical record, the six major factors that propel civilizations toward breakdown, using eclectic examples drawn from different eras and different societies. My aim is to capture the essence of each factor, not to account for the history of this or that civilization or to explain how and why the factor has become especially pressing today. Similarly, I do not deal with the exceptions that prove the rule—for instance, the geographical advantage enjoyed by the Byzantine and Ottoman empires—because I am concerned with what is common to all civilizations. Nor do I draw out at length the role and significance of these factors in the contemporary world, relying instead on the reader to reach his or her own conclusions. To describe and analyze the plight of modern civilization in depth would require a very different book (and there would be little point, because other excellent works on this topic are available[2]).

Readers of the manuscript in draft have complained that I provide a diagnosis without a cure. Surely something can be done? But new programs within the old paradigm will simply recreate the old problems in a new guise. Moreover, my analysis suggests that there is very little that we can do. Most of the trends I identify are inexorable, and complex adaptive systems are ultimately unmanageable. To the extent that we can do something, the required measures are far outside the bounds of what is feasible or even thinkable today. Indeed, as I have argued in a previous work, a genuine cure would require a revolution in human thought greater than the one that created the modern world.[3]

Such momentous changes do not occur by acts of human will. "Cultural solutions," says Wendell Berry, "are organisms, not machines, and they cannot be invented deliberately or imposed by prescription."[4] On the other hand, an honest and realistic assessment of a problem is the indispensable first step toward its solution. What follows is my best effort to provide such an assessment.

Introduction
Immoderate Greatness

> Wise men say, and not without reason, that whoever wishes to foresee the future must consult the past; for human events ever resemble those of preceding times. This arises from the fact that they are produced by men who ever have been, and ever will be, animated by the same passions, and thus they necessarily have the same results.
>
> Niccolò Machiavelli[1]

Modern civilization believes that it commands the historical process with technological power. Allied to capitalist markets that foster continual innovation, this power will allow it to overcome the challenges I identify and thereby escape the common fate of all previous civilizations. No longer bound by the past, or so we think, our future is infinitely bright. The late futurist Herman Kahn, for example, claimed that by the year 2200, "humans would everywhere be rich, numerous, and in control of the forces of nature."[2] Only a confirmed pessimist, trapped in an antiquated worldview and a pitiful ignorance of science's potential, could possibly think otherwise.

I argue to the contrary that industrial civilization will yield to the "same passions" that have produced the "same results" in all previous times. There is simply no escape from our all-too-human nature. In the end, mastering the historical process would require human beings to master themselves, something they are very far from achieving. (This is why democracy, considered by some to be an asset in the struggle against the forces that challenge industrial civilization, is in fact a liability.[3]) Commanding history would also require them to overcome all of the natural limits that have defeated previous civilizations. As will be shown, this is unlikely. Hence our civilization, too, will decline and fall. In fact, the process of decline is already well advanced.

The essential reason is contained in Gibbon's terse verdict on the decline and fall of Rome: immoderate greatness. But what exactly is immoderate greatness, and why does it foretell the downfall of civilizations?

In essence, immoderate greatness exemplifies what the ancient Greeks would have called hubris: "overbearing pride or presumption." Civilization is *Homo sapiens*'s bold attempt to rise above the natural state in which the species lived for almost all of its two hundred thousand years on Earth. Unfortunately, by its very nature, this effort to become greater encounters four implacable biophysical limits. It also sets in motion a seemingly inexorable moral and practical progression from original vigor and virtue to terminal lethargy and decadence. In other words, we can dissect hubris into its component parts and thereby specify the concrete structure of civilized man's ingrained presumption. Nevertheless, when we have done so, we shall find that the Greek answer is essentially correct. Those afflicted by hubris become the agents of their own destruction. Like a tragic hero, a civilization comes to a ruinous end due to intrinsic flaws that are the shadow side of its very virtues.

My purpose is not to propose yet another theory of historical cycles but, rather, to isolate the ecological, physical, psychological, and practical factors that drive the cycles—that is, to show that the observable rhythms and structures of human history have demonstrable causes. I do not posit an absolute determinism. The factors discussed below interact with geography, culture, and historical circumstances to create a unique trajectory for each civilization.[4] (Thus, for example, the extended survival of both the Byzantine and the Ottoman empires reflects the unique geopolitical advantages of an empire centered on the Bosporus.[5]) But these trajectories are all variations on the theme of success followed inexorably by failure.

Most historians have tended to emphasize the psychological factors as causal. Will and Ariel Durant echo Machiavelli: "History repeats itself in the large because...man is equipped to respond in stereotyped ways to frequently occurring situations and stimuli like hunger, danger, and sex."[6] Hence civilization succumbs to moral decay and practical failure. But we shall see that biophysical constraints play an equally important, if not decisive, role in propelling civilizations toward exhaustion and eventual death.

Because civilization is not natural, sustaining it entails a continuous input of matter, energy, and morale without which it would necessarily decline or even collapse. Indeed, civilization is a kind of Moloch whose demands for material and human sacrifice grow in proportion to its greatness. Looking down on Machu Picchu from the heights above, Pablo Neruda saw in its stones the ghosts of countless human beings sacrificed on the altar of civilization and cried out, "Give me back the slave you buried here!"[7] At some point the sacrifice is no longer bearable, physically or socially, so forward progress stops. As Gibbon warns, however, "all that is human must retrograde if it do not advance."[8] Thus the end of progress is necessarily the beginning of decline.[9]

The process is insidious. Limits constrict by degrees. Decay creeps in unnoticed. It is only late in the game—usually too late to do much about it—that those living become aware of a gradual and imperceptible transformation that has rendered the civilization increasingly tired, depleted, impoverished, vulnerable, and ineffectual. As Livy famously said of his own civilization:

> Rome was originally, when it was poor and small, a unique example of austere virtue; then it corrupted, it spoiled, it rotted itself by all the vices; so, little by little, we have been brought into the present condition in which we are able neither to endure the evils from which we suffer, nor the remedies we need to cure them.[10]

At last comes the implosion, as the "stupendous fabric" of an overstretched, hollowed-out, and corrupt civilization yields "to the pressure of its own weight." A barbarian invasion, a terrible plague, a devastating drought, a calamitous war, or some similar disaster is usually only the precipitating factor—the final push that causes the structure to topple. "A great civilization is not conquered from without until it has destroyed itself from within," said Will Durant.[11] Let us therefore trace the manner in which civilizations first wax immoderately great, then encounter the limits to greatness, and finally prepare their own demise.

Biophysical Limits

1
Ecological Exhaustion

> A bull contents himself with one meadow, and one forest is enough for a thousand elephants; but the little body of a man devours more than all other living creatures.
>
> Seneca[1]

> Forests precede civilizations…deserts follow them.
>
> François-René de Chateaubriand[2]

The city is an ecological parasite. It arrogates to itself matter and energy that do not naturally belong to it by sucking resources away from its hinterland. So the central institution of civilization exists, and can only exist, by systematically exploiting its rural and natural periphery. It is this exploitation that supports the higher level of social and economic complexity that characterizes civilization.[3]

Unfortunately, by their very nature, parasites debilitate or even destroy their host, so the outcome of this one-way, one-sided process is bound to be damaging in the longer term. Thus every known civilization has caused environmental harm and ecological degradation to some degree.[4] It could hardly be otherwise. Civilization is the child of the Neolithic Revolution, of the widespread adoption of agriculture as a mode of production, and agriculture necessarily causes leaching and loss of topsoil, as well as many other environmental consequences, including climate change.[5]

Nor does the city live by bread alone. It needs water, so it must build dams and aqueducts. It needs wood for fuel and timber, so it must chop down forests. It needs metal for coins, swords, and ploughshares, so it must dig mines. It needs stone to erect palaces, courts, temples, and walls, so it must quarry away mountains. And it must build the roads and ports needed to transport all the necessities of urban life. In short, a city lives by both consuming and damaging a wide array of ecological resources.

If ancient civilization had consisted of small, independent farming communities that peacefully coexisted, the damage might have been limited by the modesty of their needs. But the agricultural mode of production necessarily entailed the formation of city-states.[6] These petty polities were then inexorably incorporated into empires—cities writ large that ruthlessly mined conquered provinces for their human and natural wealth so as to increase the "greatness" of the metropolis. Thus, for example, a naked ecological imperialism was the indispensable basis of Roman wealth and power. Not surprisingly, well before the final collapse of the empire in the West, Rome left a legacy of denuded landscapes where forests once flourished or lions once roamed, and even its surviving croplands were degraded.

Although not every civilization was as bent on exploitation as the Roman Empire, the outcome was essentially the same in all cases. For it is in the nature of civilizations to wax greater. In a positive feedback loop, the ready availability of virgin resources generates a larger, wealthier population that consumes more; increased demand then spurs further resource development, and so on. Thus, little by little, renewable flow resources like forests and fisheries are overexploited, and nonrenewable stock resources like minerals are drawn down. (Growth also has other consequences that we shall explore in later chapters, but let us continue for the moment on the theme of ecological limits.)

In pursuing greatness, human beings are simply expressing their biological nature. Biological evolution is driven by the tendency of all organisms to expand their habitat and exploit the available resources—just as bacteria in a Petri dish grow until they have consumed all the nutrients and then die in a toxic soup of their own waste. Those who are the most successful in doing so win the evolutionary race. Thus we humans do what all creatures do, and we have so far been a notable success. However, as the Petri dish example suggests, the final outcome may not be so benign once we have consumed our own ecological "nutrients."

As a process, civilization resembles a long-running economic bubble. Civilizations convert found (or conquered) ecological wealth into economic goods and population growth. As the bubble expands, a spirit of "irrational exuberance" reigns. Few take thought for the morrow or consider that they are borrowing from posterity. Finally, however, resources are either effectively exhausted or no longer repay the effort needed to exploit them. As massive demand collides with dwindling supply, the ecological "credit" that has fueled expansion and created a large population accustomed to living high off the hog is choked off. The civilization begins to implode, in either a slow and measured decline or a more rapid and chaotic collapse.[7]

As civilizations encounter emerging limits, they will of course make every effort to innovate their way around them. However, as we shall see later, these efforts themselves have costs that gradually accumulate. Thus the civilization's "indebtedness" compounds. Unfortunately, the benefits accrue immediately, but the debts come due only later, so the momentum of development continues. However, at some point, "service" on the accumulated debt begins to preclude new investment, as more and more energy has to be expended simply running in place.

Stealing resources from others is not a permanent solution, because conquest, too, has serious costs: "imperial overstretch" has spelled the downfall of many empires.[8] Even peaceful trade provides no escape from biophysical limits. To get resources from others, you must normally give something valuable in return—either resources themselves, or goods and services that depend ultimately on resources.

In short, on a finite planet you cannot grow forever or violate the laws of physics. If you use renewable resources faster than they can regenerate, they will dwindle and ultimately disappear; if you produce wastes faster than they can be rendered harmless, they will poison you; and if you use nonrenewable resources to fuel current consumption, they will eventually run out. Of course, the ultimate limits are rarely reached, because diminishing returns on ecological exploitation and extraction set in well before then. Technology and good management can forestall the day of ecological reckoning, but not indefinitely.

To make matters worse, it is not resources in general that matter, for natural processes are governed by a basic ecological principle called "the law of the minimum." Thus the factor in least supply is controlling. For example, to grow cereals takes soil, seeds, fertilizer, and water as well as labor. Not only must all of these factors of production be present for there to be a crop, but they must be present in the right quality or proportion. Thin soils or poor seeds will stunt crop growth even if all the other factors are present in abundance. Thus some resources are more critical for civilization than others.

The most critical of all is water, without which life simply cannot be sustained. But as civilizations develop, they tend to overuse and misuse their water supplies, with consequences that can be serious.[9] For example, salinization due to inappropriate irrigation plagued many ancient civilizations (and continues to be a problem today). Civilizations also damage watersheds by cutting down the forests that moderate climate, promote rainfall, and store water.[10]

In addition, the law of the minimum has a corollary: consuming to the limit when times are flush leaves a civilization exposed to peril if resources decline in quality or quantity. For example, because rainfall varies from year to year, water supply inevitably fluctuates. This means that past levels of agricultural production may not always be achievable, threatening the civilization with hunger or even famine. To restate the corollary in prescriptive form, consistently pressing ecological limits is risky to the point of being suicidal.

Unfortunately, civilization does just that: as a system, its basic mode is overshoot and collapse.[11] That is, it tends to continue developing well beyond the point of ecological sense (as well as economic sense in many cases, although that is another story). In doing so, it degrades or exhausts ecological resources that are critical for its long-term survival. What ecologists call the "carrying capacity" is eroded. When the inevitable day of reckoning arrives, the civilization therefore experiences decline or even collapse until it comes into balance with the remaining, impoverished resource base.

If we ask why civilizations have consistently fallen into this trap, the answer is multifaceted. Obviously, sheer ignorance is one reason. The signs of overdevelopment are ignored until too late, so humanity only discovers the error of its ecological ways in retrospect. But there are more specific causes. Leaving the human element aside for now, one important part of the answer is that ecological costs are not reflected in economic transactions.

For instance, if ten sheep are bartered for one log, the fact that the sheep may have contributed to desertification through overgrazing, or that the tree represents ecological capital, not just the cost of felling the tree and transporting the log, is not reflected in the transaction. Thus a "market failure" has occurred: the "prices" do not represent physical reality. This failure is particularly egregious in the case of the log, for not only is the true value of an asset that took a century or more to produce not realized, but capital has also been liquidated to produce current income.

A money economy takes the disconnection, and therefore the failure, one step further. The higher the level of economic development, the more money tends to become an abstraction rather than a counter for something concrete. Thus the economy can boom as the ecology disintegrates. This is particularly true if the society resorts to currency debasement or loose credit as a way to evade encroaching physical limits and foster an artificial prosperity, for then the economy becomes completely unhinged from concrete ecological reality. Overshoot and collapse is the inevitable result.

It all seems so obvious once we step back and focus on the relation between the edifice of civilization and its ecological foundation. Of course resources are limited; of course we cannot violate limits with impunity; of course we cannot indefinitely consume natural capital. Yet history is littered with the corpses of civilizations that lived beyond their ecological means and paid the price. Why is this so? The answer is complex, and we shall deal with the psychological and sociological aspects later, but one major reason is that the human mind tends to overlook the consequences of continuous growth. Let us therefore explore the second biophysical limit confronting civilization: the exponential function.

2
Exponential Growth

> The greatest shortcoming of the human race is our inability to understand the exponential function.
>
> Albert Bartlett[1]

Why is it that civilizations have tended to see the natural world as cornucopian—that is, as a banquet on which they were free to gorge without limit? In large part this deluded view has prevailed because human beings do not readily comprehend the nature and power of exponential growth.

First, a definition: "A quantity grows *exponentially* when *its increase is proportional to what is already there*."[2] For instance, when a bank pays compound interest, the payment is added to the principal, which then becomes the basis for the next interest calculation. Thus $100 in a bank account paying 7.2 percent interest compounded annually will be worth $107.20 at the end of the first year, $114.92 at the end of the second, and so on, until the end of the tenth year when it will amount to $200.42. (A rule of thumb is that the doubling time in years is approximately equal to 72 divided by the growth rate.) And it would take only another 70 years of compounding to turn the original $100 into $25,600. Thus in just 80 years, roughly the span of a human life, the account would increase by 25,500 percent! Such is the power of the exponential function, shown vividly in the graph.

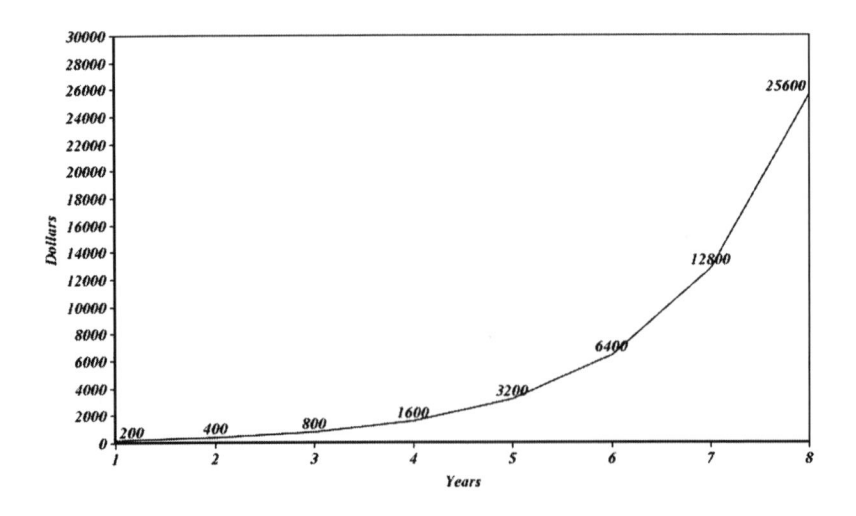

A Bank Account Compounds at 7.2 Percent

To look at the same phenomenon in another way, imagine a bacterium that divides itself in two after ten minutes. Then ten minutes later the two divide into four, and so on, to create the following progression in just the first ten doublings: 1, 2, 4, 8, 16, 32, 64, 128, 256, 512, 1024. Ten more doublings turns a thousand into a million, and ten more after that catapults a million into a billion. In just five hours, one bacterium has multiplied itself a billion times over.

An ancient Indian parable provides yet another example of the extraordinary power of compound growth. A courtier who had done the king a valuable service asked for a seemingly trivial reward: one grain of wheat on the first square of a chessboard, then two on the second, four on the third, and so on, through all of the sixty-four squares. But the king's vizier quickly calculated that to cover the board as the courtier desired would require approximately eighteen quintillion grains (i.e., eighteen followed by eighteen zeros)—an astronomically large number, greater by far than the quantity of wheat in the entire world. The wily courtier forfeited his life.

The parable reveals the manner in which the exponential function can outrun the human capacity to respond: the number of grains on the fourth square is one more than the total of all the grains on the previous three squares (1 + 2 + 4 = 7 + 1 = 8). And this same relationship holds throughout: the 128 grains on the eighth square is one more than the cumulative total placed on the previous seven squares (127). In other words, the amount required to achieve the next doubling in any series will always be *slightly larger than the sum of all previous growth.*[3]

Thus if a city of one hundred thousand inhabitants has cut down five forests for fuel since its founding and wants to keep growing, it will have to fell five more on its way to a population of two hundred thousand. Or, to put it another way, assuming the city continues growing at the same rate, then doubling the population from one hundred thousand to two hundred thousand will consume as much wood as it has used during its entire history—but in only one-sixth the time. In short, as the preceding graph illustrates, exponential growth entails ever larger increments that tend to arrive at an accelerated pace.

The same powerful arithmetic works in reverse. If the inflation rate is 3.6 percent, then a hundred years from now the purchasing power of a $1 bill will be the equivalent of only three cents today—a loss in value of 97 percent in one century. Resources are depleted in the same fashion: a mine containing one million tons of ore producing at a steady rate of ten thousand tons per annum will last a century, but if production continually increases, the ore will be exhausted in a few decades.

The lesson to be learned from these examples is that exponential growth is both insidious and explosive. It sneaks up on you and then fulminates. A simple thought experiment will further illustrate both points and highlight the attached danger.

Imagine it is 11:00 p.m., and we put a single bacterium of a species that divides once a minute into a bottle of such a size that it will be full in precisely one hour.[4] When will the bottle be half full? One minute to midnight. Now wave a magic wand and make the bottle four times bigger than it was originally. How much time have we gained? Almost none: one minute after midnight the bacteria will have grown to occupy half of the expanded bottle, and they will fill it completely a minute later.

Starting with a much larger bottle is not a real solution, because the increments of growth are now overwhelming. A bottle thirty-two times larger than the original will be full at five minutes past midnight. Even a bottle one thousand times larger will fill up by ten past midnight! In other words, a magic wand only delays the inevitable: exponential growth is a tsunami that sweeps all before it.

Now suppose that it is imperative to keep the original bottle from filling up. When would we need to step in to stop the bacteria from multiplying? At five minutes to midnight, the bacteria would occupy a mere 3 percent of the bottle, so why should we worry? Even a quarter-full bottle might not alarm us, for there would seem to be ample time to respond—although it is now two minutes to midnight. But if we wait until the bottle is half full, the situation is desperate: we have only one minute to act.

To reiterate, exponential growth is both insidious and explosive. Like a tsunami, its gathering energy goes unnoticed until the water rises up and overwhelms those on the shore. How soon the impact of growth will become overwhelming is a function of the growth rate in relation to the limits of the system, as well as of the society's management skills and technological prowess. However, since waxing greater is wired into the genes of civilization, the issue is not if, but when growth assumes the proportions of a tsunami.

Nor is technology a panacea. As we saw above, making the bottle larger by several orders of magnitude does not solve the problem. It only postpones the day of reckoning—and briefly at that. In fact, technology is a double-edged sword. On the one hand, it amplifies the civilization's resource base and therefore enables growth to continue. On the other hand, precisely because it does allow growth to continue, it raises the stakes of the game. For if each doubling requires a quantity of resources equal to all that the civilization has consumed hitherto, then there must come a point when it will no longer be possible to supply it.[5]

There are two additional reasons why civilizations tend to be blindsided by exponential growth, and both have to do with human psychology. One is a holdover from the Paleolithic past, and the other a more recent acquisition (although it, too, is influenced by that past).

The human mind is still fundamentally Paleolithic. That is, it was hardwired by evolution for the life of a hunter-gatherer on the African savannah, a life centered on day-to-day survival in small bands of intimates and kinsmen. In practice, this means that human beings excel at concrete perception but are much less adept at abstraction. And they are quick to perceive the immediate and dramatic but likely to overlook long-term trends and consequences. They are therefore strongly present-oriented and tend to neglect or devalue the future.

The upshot is that the human mind is not well equipped for the cognitive demands of civilized life in general, and it is singularly ill equipped to deal with the implications of exponential growth in particular.[6] The penchant for human societies to lurch from crisis to crisis arises from these facts. By the time the average human being recognizes the existence of a problem, it is already one minute to midnight.

But haven't we moderns transcended our Paleolithic roots by becoming more rational? Yes, but only recently and only in part. Mostly we use rationality in the service of our primal drives—that is, instrumentally, so as to become greater. Moreover, rationality by itself does not guarantee greater foresight. To the contrary, as any economist will be happy to explain, the "discounted value" of the future is effectively zero.

Returning to the inflation example above, we can see why. At a discount rate of 3.6 percent, the "present value" of a dollar a hundred years from now is only 3 cents. Anything that far in the future is therefore worthless for all practical purposes, and even events just a decade or two away are heavily discounted by a "rational" economic actor. Thus the rationalist joins the savage in devaluing the future.

Although the logic is irrefutable, the flaw in the reasoning lies precisely in the term "present value," which reveals that the economist is still a caveman at heart. It is *now* that matters—not next year, let alone twenty or a hundred years from now. So industrial civilization quite "rationally" burns through its stocks of fossil fuels, even though a moment's reflection shows that they will be much more valuable in the future.[7]

Moreover, even if people sense that something is not quite right—civilization has gotten too big, too complex, too hard to manage—they may still not see that the problems are caused in large part by exponential growth and that the solution therefore lies in controlling that growth, not in programs or technologies designed to allow it to continue. For if you remove one constraint, renewed growth quickly pushes the civilization up against the next one, and so on, until it buckles under the strain.

Some will object that such pessimism is unwarranted. It may be that previous civilizations have faced insurmountable limits, but that cannot be true of modern industrial civilization. For we are unique in possessing powerful technologies that will allow the human race to expand the Earth's carrying capacity indefinitely and thereby forever outrun exponential growth. In other words, we can increase the size of the bottle virtually without limit and fulfill Herman Kahn's forecast: humanity "everywhere…rich, numerous, and in control of the forces of nature."

But this is a dream. We do not, in fact, possess the means to make civilization ever greater, for even the most powerful technology cannot flout or evade the laws of nature. In addition, technology has a shadow side—it destroys more than it creates. To see why, we now turn to the third biophysical barrier confronting civilization: the entropy law.

3
Expedited Entropy

> If someone points out to you that your pet theory of the universe is in disagreement with Maxwell's equations—then so much the worse for Maxwell's equations. If it is found to be contradicted by observation—well, these experimentalists do bungle things sometimes. But if your theory is found to be against the second law of thermodynamics I can give you no hope; there is nothing for it but to collapse in deepest humiliation.
>
> Sir Arthur Stanley Eddington[1]

The laws of thermodynamics, among the most basic known to science, constitute a natural tyranny against which resistance is useless. They guarantee that the human "conquest" of nature is, and always will be, a Pyrrhic victory. But what are these laws that so decisively set aside the human pretension to technological dominance?

The First Law states that energy is always conserved. It can change form, but it can neither be created nor destroyed. However, the Second Law states that entropy tends to increase (where entropy is a measure of chaos, randomness, and disorder). In layman's terms, this means that energy tends to decay into less and less useful forms. In practice, therefore, every transformation of energy from one form to another incurs a loss. There may be just as much total energy after the transformation as before, but the quality of that energy will be poorer.

In their purest scientific form, the laws of thermodynamics are concerned with energy as heat and do not seem at first glance to have much to do with daily life. In fact, however, they govern every aspect of the natural and human economies. It takes energy to perform work, to effect the transformation of matter or energy from one form into another, and all such transformations incur the losses ordained by the Second Law.

One way of restating the Second Law, often called the entropy law, is to say that matter-energy transformations cannot be reversed; time's arrow flies in only one direction. Thus when Humpty Dumpty takes his great fall, all the king's horses and all the king's men can never put him together again. His material "energy" has been irretrievably lost. Similarly, when ice melts in a glass of lemonade, the cold "energy" stored in the ice cubes dissipates into the environment, never to be recaptured. And, of course, vice versa for hot objects. For instance, our sun is slowly but surely radiating away its concentrated energy. Approximately five billion years from now, it will exhaust its fuel and eventually fade into a dim ember. In short, over time energy moves inexorably downhill from a more useful or concentrated state to one that is less useful or concentrated. This movement is called entropy.

Unfortunately, civilization expedites entropy. For example, agricultural production is the foundation of civilized life. But the word production is a misnomer, for what humans actually do is mine the topsoil. Virgin soil is a complex ecosystem developed over millennia that contains a myriad of chemical elements and biological beings within a very specific physical structure. Humanity breaks into this ecological climax to profit from the rich store of energy that it contains. The product is food for human consumption—but the byproduct is erosion, compaction, leaching, and other damage to the soil's vitality and integrity. And the nutrients in the food are not usually returned to the land but instead excreted into latrines and sewers, whence they are dispersed into rivers, lakes, and oceans never to be recaptured (except in the negative form of pollution). Thus the entropy of the system has increased. The originally rich topsoil has become poorer or has even eroded away, and the wider environment has also been impoverished.[2]

Over the centuries, farmers have learned to counteract the worst entropic consequences of agriculture by various means: crop rotation, fallowing, terracing, manuring, and the like. These measures do indeed slow down the losses. In fact, given favorable circumstances it is possible to construct systems of sustainable agriculture that keep entropic losses to a bare minimum. Such systems are necessarily labor intensive and scrupulously conservative—more like horticulture than our usual notion of agriculture. For instance, traditional rice farmers in some parts of Asia were able to achieve a relatively stable, man-made agricultural climax (by using night soil, among other measures).[3]

In most cases, however, conditions are not so favorable. Moreover, given the propensity of civilizations to grow both in population and appetite, demand for agricultural products is bound to increase. Since the land in its natural state is incapable of meeting this increased demand, external energy must be applied to boost yields artificially. Thus entropy increases, as the quantity of energy consumed per unit of output rises higher. This development reaches its apex in industrialized agriculture, which is a biological machine that turns petroleum into calories at a ratio of approximately ten to one.[4] In other words, the entropic price of modern man's bowl of porridge is the degradation of at least ten times as much energy as is contained in the bowl itself.

Or take one of the great inventions of civilization: the bath. Whether it is the Roman *thermae*, the Arab *hammam*, or the traditional Japanese *furo*, they were all heated with wood. But in the process most of the energy in the wood was wasted. That is, it turned into smoke, ashes, and heat—some of which did the work of making hot water, but most of which escaped up the chimney. And even the useful heat in the bath water was soon dissipated into the atmosphere, just like the cold in the glass of lemonade. In addition, it took matter and energy to build the baths in the first place and to maintain them thereafter (not to mention aqueducts, roads, and other supportive infrastructure). Creating the amenity that elevates civilization over savagery therefore involves converting concentrated energy and matter into useless waste products, while extracting a modicum of useful work along the way.

A contemporary example will illustrate the point more concretely and also make clear why technology cannot forever overcome the limits imposed by thermodynamics. When coal is burned to produce electricity, only about 35 percent of the energy in the coal is converted into electrical energy. The rest becomes waste heat, various gases (such as carbon dioxide), various chemicals (such as sulfuric acid), particulates, and ash. And even the electricity dissipates into the environment as waste heat once it has done its work. From the physicist's point of view, the books are balanced—there is just as much matter and energy in the overall system as before—but what remains is significantly lower in quality. The upshot is that for every unit of good that man creates using this particular technology, he manufactures two units of bad—and even the good is ephemeral.

Could we improve on this? Yes, but not as much as we might like. Looking at systems in general, a two to one ratio of loss to gain is actually quite good; a ratio of ten to one, as in industrial agriculture, is more typical in non-mechanical systems. And improvement in mechanical systems soon encounters diminishing returns (which means that it takes a leap to an entirely new technology to make substantial progress).

To revert to our example, generating electricity from coal-fired plants is a mature technology, so any thermodynamic gains would likely be modest. However, even a magic wand would be of little use in this case. Perfect efficiency is impossible, for that would be tantamount to perpetual motion, which the entropy law forbids. But even if we were able to raise efficiency to the thermodynamic maximum of 77 percent, this only represents a doubling—and, as we know from the previous chapter, one doubling buys one minute of exponential time.

In addition, technological improvements actually increase thermodynamic costs. Take the substitution of the automobile for the horse. To make a horse requires a modest investment in pasture, water, and fodder for the two to three years it takes from conception until the horse can work. But to make a car requires not only many direct inputs—steel, copper, fuel, water, chemicals, and so forth—but also many indirect ones such as a factory and labor force as well as the matter and energy needed to sustain them. To use a technical term, the "embodied energy" in the car is many times that in the horse. In addition, the thermodynamic cost of operating the car is far greater. A horse needs only a modicum of hay, water, and oats procured locally without too much difficulty. But the auto requires oil wells, refineries, tankers, gasoline stations, mechanics' shops, and so on—that is, a myriad of direct inputs that are difficult and expensive to procure, as well as a host of indirect costs. So the substitution of auto for horse may have brought many advantages, but at a heavy thermodynamic price.

Even the technological leap represented by the computer is no different. Its partisans may believe that it will be the instrument of humanity's final liberation from the tyranny of nature, but a quick glance at the enormous quantity of embodied energy in each computer and in the systems that support it, plus the major energy requirements needed to operate networks, testify otherwise. The idea that technology will allow us to do ever more with ever less is a delusion. The more humanity resorts to technology, the more it expedites entropy (and generates other problems that we shall take up in the next chapter).

It is vital to understand that technology is not a *source* of energy. That is, it is not a fuel in its own right, only a means for putting fuel to work or for transforming one energy resource into another. Thus, for example, coal can be converted into gasoline—but at a high thermodynamic price, because much of the potential energy in the coal is lost in the process. Or technology can make the conversion of energy more efficient—but, as we have seen, only up to a point. (Moreover, gains in efficiency tend to be nullified by increases in demand, a phenomenon known as Jevons Paradox.) Similarly, technology can make new energy resources available—but only by expending energy to find and exploit them. So technology does not make energy out of thin air. On the contrary, technology is always ultimately *dependent* on the supply of energy. If the quantity or quality of energy resources dwindles, the power of technology declines along with them.

Above all, technology depends critically on energy density. The total amount of available energy is staggering, but very little of it is available in concentrated form. That is the beauty of fossil fuels. They are the energy-dense residue of past solar energy in the form of buried organic matter that has been subjected to eons of geological heat and pressure. With such a concentrated source of energy, technology can perform wonders, because it is, in effect, traveling thermodynamically downhill from dense to diffuse—from coal to electricity and waste heat, instead of vice versa. By contrast, dispersed energy can do much less work and therefore limits what technology can do. Solar rays will make hot water for a household but do not lend themselves to running a large power plant.

True, technology can concentrate dispersed energy but only by traveling thermodynamically uphill from diffuse to dense. To illustrate the challenge, imagine trying to recover the approximately 15,000 tons of gold dissolved in seawater. Although technically feasible, the capital and energy cost of turning atoms into ingots would be prohibitive.

Thus one of the best ways of understanding the relationship of energy, entropy, and technology is by examining economic systems in terms of net energy—that is, how much energy remains after subtracting the cost of effecting the transformation. The technical term is *energy return on investment* or EROI (also known as EROEI for energy return on energy invested). As we have seen, the EROI of industrial agriculture is negative: it takes ten units in to get one unit out. The return on other technologies is not so easy to calculate. How does one value the advantages of the automobile against its very high entropic costs, except by saying that the horse is far less expensive in thermodynamic terms?

In some cases, however, there is a clear numerical progression. It used to be that it took the energetic equivalent of only one barrel of petroleum to obtain a hundred barrels—that is, an EROI of one hundred to one. But this ratio has now declined to roughly fifteen to one and is destined to fall even further, because the remaining resources are on the whole more difficult, dangerous, and expensive to extract and refine.[5] Hence the mere quantity of a resource is not what is important. A billion barrels of oil in the ground may sound like a lot, but if it costs five hundred million barrels to extract and refine, then the net energy is only five hundred million barrels, and the EROI is just two to one.

Because quality, not quantity, is the critical issue, the current debate over so-called peak oil is often incoherent. The real concern for a civilization dependent on fossil fuels is not really the moment in time when the maximum rate of petroleum extraction is reached, after which production enters terminal decline, but rather the inexorable trend toward lower net energy and higher costs, both monetary and environmental. New discoveries and improved techniques may boost production in the short term, but to hail them as refutations of peak oil while ignoring the long-term trend toward lower net energy makes no sense. (In addition, exponential growth in demand makes even "elephant" discoveries of little import.[6])

Low net energy is why most of the schemes for replacing fossil fuels with one or another form of ambient solar energy on a scale that would satisfy current demand, much less future growth, will come to naught; the EROI will be marginal, and the capital costs exorbitant. In addition, the law of the minimum applies. For instance, many "unconventional" fossil-fuel projects require water to enable the process, often in large quantities, and water is already becoming scarce. To reiterate, unless it is a matter of simply scooping up found wealth, technology is not a panacea. It is dogged at every step by the laws of thermodynamics.

Perhaps the best way to understand the impact of the entropy law on human affairs is to use a pointed analogy. Nature operates what is, in effect, an extremely onerous tax system. Even the latter days of the Roman Empire, when people fled cities in droves to escape the taxman, seem benign by comparison. For every matter-energy transaction has to pay a thermodynamic tax that is greater by far than the value of the transaction itself. Thus, for instance, nature taxes the conversion of coal into electricity at a rate of roughly 200 percent!

However, the tax is for the most part unseen, and it is not usually paid immediately. Or, to put it another way, some reap the benefits of the transaction and succeed in shoving the costs off onto others: other species, other places, other classes, other generations pay the tax. Hence the tendency is for a civilization to continue developing despite an accumulating thermodynamic debt load. At some point, however, the taxman presents his bill. "Progress" then ceases, and the civilization finds itself in dire straits.

Civilization is trapped in a thermodynamic vicious circle from which escape is well nigh impossible. The greater a civilization becomes, the more the citizens produce and consume—but the more they produce and consume, the larger the increase in entropy. The longer economic development continues, the more depletion, decay, degradation, and disorder accumulate in the system as a whole, even if it brings a host of short-term benefits. Depending on a variety of factors—the quantity and quality of available resources, the degree of technological and managerial skill, and so forth—the process can continue for some time but not indefinitely. At some point, just as in the ecological realm, a civilization exhausts its thermodynamic "credit" and begins to implode.

The only way out would be radically to transform civilization so that the human economy resembled the natural economy. Nature is highly efficient in thermodynamic terms. The steady flow of solar energy is not simply consumed but is instead used to build up a rich and diverse capital stock. To put it more technically, nature internalizes thermodynamic costs, using the same matter and energy over and over to wring a maximum of life out of a minimum of energy.

Although it might be theoretically possible for the human economy to mimic the natural economy, it would involve a radical transformation of civilization as we know it. Societies would have to be far more intricately and closely coupled—just as in natural ecosystems. And individuals would have to tolerate strong checks on human will and desire—that is, powerful negative feedback, just as in natural ecosystems. But even if such a hive-like existence were somehow acceptable, one would have to question whether human beings have the managerial capacity to sustain it. Let us, therefore, turn to the fourth biophysical limit that confronts civilization: the challenge of complexity.

4
Excessive Complexity

> Species, people, firms, governments are all complex entities that must survive in dynamic environments that evolve over time. Their ability to understand such environments is inherently limited.... These limits are a fundamental feature of [all complex] systems [and] can no more be overcome by smarter analysis than we are able to break binding physical constraints, such as our inability to travel faster than the speed of light. This is why things fail.
>
> Paul Ormerod[1]

> Self-organizing, nonlinear, feedback systems are inherently unpredictable. They are not controllable. They are understandable only in the most general way.... Our science itself, from quantum theory to the mathematics of chaos, leads us into irreducible uncertainty.
>
> Donella H. Meadows[2]

Civilization may be a problem too hard for the human brain to solve. As previously noted, our Paleolithic nervous system was cobbled together by evolution to meet the relatively simple demands of living in small bands of hunter-gatherers. Because we are a clever generalist species, we have nonetheless managed to adapt reasonably well to civilized life. However, once civilization becomes too complex, that adaptation begins to break down—politically, socially, and managerially. (In this chapter, we shall deal with the latter and leave the political and social aspects for later.) But given the tendency of civilizations to wax greater, they inevitably do become more complex. Thus unless the progression toward greater complexity is interrupted by outside forces, they must eventually reach the point of breakdown.

A homely metaphor will illustrate the point. A juggler, no matter how dedicated and skilled, can only handle only so many balls. Add even one more, and he loses control. Now imagine that same juggler trying to keep his own balls in the air while simultaneously fielding and throwing balls from and to multiple others. That is roughly the situation in a complex civilization: many millions of individuals and entities are engaged in a mass, mutual juggling act. How likely is it that there will be no dropped balls? And how will it be possible to keep adding balls and participants and not overload the system so that it begins to break down?

Complexity is not something nebulous. It can be quantified, says Joseph Tainter:

> Complexity is generally understood to refer to such things as the size of a society, the number and distinctiveness of its parts, the variety of specialized social roles that it incorporates, the number of distinct social personalities present, and the variety of mechanisms for organizing these into a coherent, functioning whole. Augmenting any of these dimensions increases the complexity of a society. Hunter-gatherer societies (by way of illustrating one contrast in complexity) contain no more than a few dozen distinct social personalities, while modern European censuses recognize 10,000 to 20,000 unique occupational roles, and industrial soci-

eties may contain overall more than 1,000,000 different kinds of social personalities.[3]

The problem of managing complexity has two major aspects. The first is sheer overload. Thanks to the exponential function, as civilizations grow the number of balls that need to be juggled escalates. Add in the difficulty of dealing with ecological exhaustion and diminishing thermodynamic returns, and the problem is bound to become overwhelming in the long run. The civilization's very greatness makes it unwieldy—hard to control and harder still to change. At some point, it is likely to encounter what Thomas Homer-Dixon calls an "ingenuity gap."[4] The human ability to cope lags the accumulating problems, until the chasm between the demand for ingenuity and the supply of it can no longer be bridged.

Overload is not merely quantitative. As Tainter points out, solving the problems of population growth, resource use, and so forth is the very business of civilization. Hence "there is persistent pressure for complexity to increase"; for the never-ending succession of problems can only be solved "by developing more complex technologies, establishing new institutions, adding more specialists or bureaucratic levels to an institution, increasing organization or regulation, or gathering and processing more information."[5] Thus:

> For the past 12,000 years human societies have seemed almost inexorably to grow more complex. For the most part this has been successful: complexity confers advantages, and one of the reasons for our success as a species has been our ability to increase rapidly the complexity of our behavior.[6]

Unfortunately, says Tainter, these advantages have a societal price that increases over time, for "as easier solutions are exhausted, problem solving moves inexorably to greater complexity, higher costs, and diminishing returns."[7] Indeed, simply maintaining the attained level of complexity in infrastructure, in regulation, and in expertise begins to consume more and more resources—human resources, capital resources, material resources—meaning that the society has to run harder and harder just to stay in the same place.[8] Moreover, problems that were once separate begin to coalesce into a "problematique," a nexus of problems that mutually aggravate each other.

The historical record evinces a clear trend toward declining marginal returns on the human investment in civilized complexity. The investment yields relatively large gains at first, but as the level of complexity increases, the gains gradually diminish and may even turn negative. To borrow the image of Tyler Cowen, once the low-hanging fruit has been plucked, what is left are the slimmer pickings of small marginal improvements and eventual stagnation.[9]

Thus ancient Rome's "investment" in conquest brought it great profit at first but increasing costs thereafter, until the empire became more burden than benefit. And measures intended to preserve it—such as, building expensive walls and hiring mercenaries to man them or imposing higher taxes and stricter regulations—only hastened the empire's demise (in the West).

Modern civilization offers numerous examples of diminishing returns. We have already seen that extracting energy resources has become more difficult, dangerous, and expensive and will become even more so in the future. We picked the low-hanging fruit first and must now scrabble for smaller, poorer, or dirtier deposits in hostile locations.

Similarly, investing in primary schools to produce a literate and numerate population costs little compared to the enormous social and economic benefit that results. But highly specialized and technical postgraduate education, however necessary to meet the needs of a more complex society, is both far more expensive and much less beneficial in proportion to the expense.

In the same way, relatively simple and inexpensive public health measures dramatically increase life spans, whereas high-priced medical technology may extend the life of a few individuals but provides little benefit to the general population. Indeed, it entails dramatically increased social costs—and it may even, or so many observers believe, inflict more suffering than it relieves on the putative beneficiaries.[10]

What these examples illustrate is that complexity is a function of energy. We like to think that we have attained our current level of complexity through sheer scientific prowess. But this is at best a half-truth. It takes vast energy resources to implement the technological solutions that enable our complexity. For example, we have already seen that the enormous "productivity" of industrial agriculture is a sham. It is a machine for converting ten calories of fossil-fuel energy into one calorie of food.

Thus if the quantity or quality of available energy declines significantly—either because of supply problems or because more energy is required to achieve the same ends—the civilization is in trouble. It can no longer afford its attained level of complexity and must either simplify itself until complexity and energy are once again in balance, or it must, like the Romans, squeeze more out of its resource base than can be sustained over the long term, which simply postpones the inevitable. In short, because energy is the sine qua non of complexity, anything that diminishes the quantity, quality, or efficiency of energy threatens a complex civilization's survival.

One of the worst consequences of growing complexity is the bureaucratic hypertrophy made famous by C. Northcote Parkinson: fewer naval bottoms on the high seas, many more human bottoms on chairs in the Admiralty.[11] But as the number of functionaries increases out of proportion to the tasks to be performed, government becomes more and more unwieldy and expensive. Onerous taxes and stifling regulations follow as a matter of course, so initiative and enterprise are strangled in red tape. Eventually the growing burden of problems caused by previous solutions becomes insupportable, and the civilization declines.

Civilizations are trapped in a vicious circle. They must keep solving the problems of complexity, for that is the price of civilized existence, but every solution creates new, ever more difficult problems, which then require new, ever more demanding solutions. Thus complexity breeds more of the same, and each increase in complexity makes it harder to cope, while at the same time escalating the penalty for failure. In effect, civilizations enact a tragedy in which their raison d'être—the use of energy to foster the complexity that raises them above the hunter-gatherer level of subsistence—becomes the agent of their ultimate downfall.

The second major aspect of the complexity management problem is that unpredictability and uncontrollability increase with every increment of growth, usually disproportionately. The problem is not just that sheer quantitative change begins to overload the jugglers' capacity or even that complexity increases in proportion. Beyond a certain point, growth leads to a fundamental, qualitative change in the nature of systems.

Specifically, it leads to what scientists call "chaos," meaning that a system is characterized by so many feedback loops operating in a nonlinear fashion that its behavior becomes more and more impenetrable and unpredictable and therefore less and less manageable, because neither the timing nor the severity of specific events is foreseeable. Complex adaptive systems can be more or less stable and robust, but as physicist

Per Bak warns, "Complexity is criticality."[12] Thus increasing the complexity of a civilization inexorably pushes it toward the critical end of the spectrum, meaning that both the challenges and the risks of managing its systems begin to compound.

In fact, complex adaptive systems cannot be managed in the usual sense of that word. "An actor in a complex system controls almost nothing," says Scott Page, yet "influences almost everything."[13] Just understanding system behavior, let alone controlling it, challenges the human mind. As Meadows points out, our minds and language are linear and sequential, but systems happen all at once and overwhelm us intellectually:

> Systems surprise us because our minds like to think about single causes neatly producing single effects. We like to think about one or at most a few things at a time.... But we live in a world in which many causes routinely come together to produce many effects.[14]

In addition, because system behavior is the result of deep structures, it cannot be understood or explained without resorting to sophisticated models. Conventional forms of analysis are simply not up to the job. But, as the epigraphs to this chapter point out, even "smarter analysis" is no match for the "irreducible uncertainty" of systems.

In short, limited, fallible human beings are bound to bungle the job of managing complex systems. What they can neither understand nor predict, they cannot expect to control, so failure is inevitable at some point.

The tedious repetition of financial crises provides a perfect illustration. The financial system is the epitome of a chaotic system, and generation after generation of highly motivated, talented, and well-capitalized individuals in both the public and private sectors have time and again failed to prevent intoxicating booms from becoming devastating busts—and this despite the lessons of economic history, which are quite well understood.[15] Of course, manias, panics, and crashes are the consequence not just of intellectual error but, as we shall see in later chapters, of other human shortcomings as well. However, intellectual error alone is sufficient to cause practical failure.

By way of illustration, systems analysts have found that company executives, legislators, and other decision makers often have a cogent grasp of the problem that needs to be solved and are usually committed to solving it—that is, they are not simply looking for an easy way out—but they miss the solution, because it is "counterintuitive" (i.e., surprising to the linear mind). In fact, says Meadows, even when they have identified with great accuracy the best leverage point, "more often than not they push the change in the *wrong direction*."[16] In other words, they typically respond in ways that will make the problem worse. For example, the farm subsidies intended to preserve family farming actually promote agribusiness instead.[17] And the ill-advised actions and policies that create financial crises are too often followed by equally ill-advised remedies that exacerbate them.

In addition, because human beings cannot easily comprehend non-linear systems with their linear minds, they repeatedly fall into a host of "systems traps" identified by Meadows—to wit, mistaking symptoms for causes, bounded rationality, the blame game, tugs of war, policy resistance, the tragedy of the commons, a drift to low performance, escalation, competitive exclusion, addiction, and rule beating.[18] One of the greatest traps of all is fanaticism: refusing to reconsider the values and goals of the system, even though they have now become perverse or even disastrous.[19] Sadly, therefore, those charged with managing complex systems are all too likely to behave in ways that grease the skids for decline and possible collapse.

In fact, the potential for catastrophe is ever present in chaotic systems. The gradual accumulation of small changes can push a system over an unseen threshold and thereby precipitate rapid and radical change. For example, once overexploitation causes fish stocks to decline below a critical, but unquantifiable, level they can no longer reproduce. Similarly, seemingly small causes can nevertheless have dramatic effects, as when a slight change in water temperature in the Western Pacific Ocean triggers an El Niño event that brings torrential rain to South America and anomalous weather to other parts of the world.

In addition, the very fact that complex systems have key links and nodes connected by multiple feedback loops means that they are vulnerable to a cascade of failure. To put it another way, systems that are too tightly coupled or too efficient are fragile; they lack resilience. That is how region-wide electrical outages propagate. The failure of one sector brings down another and another until the grid itself fails, and once down it takes heroic effort to get it up and running again.

What is worse, societies struggling with the dilemmas of complexity risk being toppled by what Homer-Dixon calls "synchronous failure."[20] When formerly separate problems coalesce into a problematique, the society does not face one or two discrete challenges, as in simpler times, but instead a swarm of simultaneous challenges that can overwhelm the society's capacity to respond, thereby provoking a general collapse (i.e., a catastrophe that propagates rapidly across a globe that is ever more tightly coupled).

Dire implications follow directly from seeing civilizations as chaotic in the scientific sense. Complex adaptive systems are stable until they are overstressed. Then one perturbation too many, or one that arrives at the wrong moment, can tip the system into instability virtually overnight, with unpredictable and frequently distressing consequences. As Will Durant noted, "From barbarism to civilization requires a century; from civilization to barbarism needs but a day."[21] Thus, says Niall Ferguson, the standard historian's view of decline and fall—that it is a relatively gentle and gradual process—is too sanguine:

> Empires do not in fact appear, rise, reign, decline, and fall according to some recurrent and predictable life cycle. It is historians who retrospectively portray the process of imperial dissolution as slow-acting, with multiple overdetermining causes. Rather, empires behave like all complex adaptive systems. They function in apparent equilibrium for some unknowable period. And then, quite abruptly, they collapse.... [T]he shift from consummation to destruction and then to desolation is not cyclical. It is sudden.[22]

The second implication is even more distressing to contemplate: there may be no way to reform an advanced civilization. Complex adaptive systems operate according to their own inner dynamic, which can only be imperfectly understood by the human mind or influenced by human conduct. Once a civilization is plagued by numerous intractable problems, most attempts at reform will therefore either fail or make matters worse. Indeed, ironically, it may be the very effort to reform that precipitates the collapse. It was *perestroika* and *glasnost* that allowed the stupendous fabric of the USSR to implode. Similarly, it was Louis XVI's convening of the Estates-General that triggered the revolution and regicide that liquidated the *ancien régime*.[23]

As these examples suggest, the timing and trajectory of collapse are essentially unpredictable and uncontrollable. Hence planning to avoid breakdown or to make a gentle and controlled transition from one stable state to another may be next to impossible. That does not mean that planning is useless. As all generals learn, war plans never survive first contact with the enemy, but planning is nonetheless an indispensable preparation for battle. However, it does mean that a gentle and gradual transition that goes according to plan is highly unlikely. In effect, chaos sets at naught the human pretension to mastery of the historical process.

By way of summary, the complexity that is the essence of civilization is utterly dependent on a continuous input of physical, intellectual, and moral energy without which it simply cannot be sustained. But even this is not enough. In the end, to the extent that it can be done at all, managing a complex system requires prudence—that is, the exercise of judgment, caution, forethought, and self-restraint.

Indeed, the real product of genuine systems analysis is not solutions but wisdom. To wit, understanding that excessive complexity is both costly and perilous and that management in the sense of control is unachievable. This would lead us to see that the proper (or only) way to "manage" civilization is by *not allowing it to become too complex*—in fact, deliberately designing in restraints, redundancy, and resiliency, even if the price is less power, freedom, efficiency, or profit than we might otherwise gain through greater complexity. To revert to our financial metaphor, to prevent busts, one must stop booms from happening in the first place by taking away the punchbowl of credit well before the party has gotten out of hand. So wisdom consists in consciously renouncing "immoderate greatness."

Unfortunately, although naturally clever, human beings are not innately wise, especially in crowds.[24] Hence they pursue greatness instead of renouncing it, and any attempt to take away the punchbowl meets with fierce resistance. It is certainly conceivable that we could learn to do better. After all, any peasant knows that judicious pruning (i.e., reducing the complexity of trees) increases the health and yield of his orchard. So why don't we prudently check the growth of our civilization and prune back our level of complexity to achieve resilience and sustainability? Alas, we never have. Rather, humanity seems fated to commit the same errors over and over, as the "same passions" inexorably produce "the same results." So let us now turn to what keeps human beings from acting wisely to preserve their civilization from decline and fall.

Human Error

5
Moral Decay

> I must study politics and war, that our sons may have liberty to study mathematics and philosophy. Our sons ought to study mathematics and philosophy, geography, natural history and naval architecture, navigation, commerce and agriculture in order to give their children the right to study painting, poetry, music, architecture, statuary, tapestry and porcelain.
>
> John Adams[1]

At first glance, Adams's aspiration seems laudable. After all, what is the point of civilization if not to become "civilized"? But if all the grandchildren are poets, painters, and connoisseurs, who then will man the ramparts, dig the mines, build the dams, run the factories, keep the accounts, or teach the children? In other words, dirty their hands doing the hard and necessary work of preserving the civilization's political, social, economic, and technological base? Yet precisely this progression from dutiful soldier to effete poet—from vigor and virtue to decadence and decay—has been a factor in the decline of every known civilization.

That civilizations decline has been understood since ancient times. Many historians, philosophers, seers, and poets have attempted to describe the cycle of history and capture its driving forces. Hesiod, Plato, Polybius, Ibn Khaldun, Giambattista Vico, Gustave Le Bon,

Oswald Spengler, Pitirim Sorokin, and Arnold Toynbee are just a few of the most noted. And there is general agreement among them that the decline is intimately related to the decay of the civilization's moral core or guiding ideal. However, none have captured the course of decline quite so succinctly as Sir John Bagot Glubb, better known by his *nom de guerre* Glubb Pasha.[2]

In Glubb's view, the history of civilizations describes an arc that starts with an Age of Pioneers (or Conquests) and then moves successively through the Ages of Commerce, Affluence, and Intellect before terminating in an Age of Decadence. Two implacable forces propel this movement. First, in a process analogous to ecological succession, each age creates socioeconomic conditions favorable to the emergence of the next. Second, each new generation therefore grows up in altered circumstances that foster a changed way of thinking and acting. The outcome is a positive feedback loop in which changed material conditions engender mental changes that foster still more material change, and so on, until the civilization declines into decadence.

The Age of Pioneers is characterized by "unresting enterprise" and "fearless initiative." Because "glory and honour [are] the principal objects of ambition," conquistadors "hack their way through jungles, climb mountains, or brave the oceans in tiny cockle-shells" pursuing them. "Abound[ing] in courage, energy and initiative," they overcome every obstacle to found an empire, often overwhelming more numerous and better armed opponents by sheer élan. Having done so, the pioneers quickly appropriate the most useful aspects of conquered or neighboring cultures to achieve state-of-the-art military, technological, and administrative sophistication. But they maintain their pioneer virtues—above all, optimism, confidence, devotion to duty, a sense of honor, a shared purpose, and adherence to a strict moral code.[3] Succinctly put, morale is high and consensus strong.

The consequence of imperial rule is political stability over a wide geographic area as well as general economic conditions favorable for manufacture and trade. As the merchant class grows wealthier, it gradually appropriates more and more of the prestige and power belonging to soldiers and statesmen. An Age of Commerce therefore succeeds the Age of Pioneers. During the first half of this new phase, says Glubb, "The ancient virtues of courage, patriotism and devotion to duty are still in evidence. The nation is proud, united and full of self-confidence." In addition, "daring initiative is shown in the search for profitable enterprises in the far corners of the earth, perpetuating to some degree the adventurous courage of the Age of Conquests."

This happy combination of adventurous courage and commercial prowess cannot last. As wealth piles up, the populace is gradually seduced by riches and softened by luxury.[4] "Money replaces honour and adventure as the objective of the best young men," and an Age of Affluence succeeds the Age of Commerce.

The civilization is now at its peak. "The immense wealth accumulated in the nation dazzles the onlookers, [and enough] of the ancient virtues of courage, energy and patriotism survive" to make the society seem both glorious and impregnable. But beneath the surface, greed and selfishness crowd out the ideals of duty and service. In addition, success breeds hubris in the form of complacency, arrogance, self-righteousness, and over-confidence. A spoiled society begins to rot from within.

One symptom of rot is increased defensiveness. "Immensely rich [and] no longer interested in glory or duty," the populace thinks primarily of hanging on to what they already have and loses all appetite for conquest or even war. The prospect of dying for one's country is no longer *dulce et decorum*, but odious and absurd. So the society buys off enemies or hires mercenaries when fighting cannot be avoided. It even makes a moral virtue of martial reluctance: "Military readiness, or aggressiveness, is denounced as primitive and immoral."

Another symptom of rot is an increasing focus on welfare—social insurance, medical care, charitable works, and the like. Affluence fosters a sense of entitlement, as well as a feeling that none should be left behind. The upshot is a welfare state with a burgeoning roster of clients and a growing burden of subsidies, along with a corresponding loss of personal responsibility and independence.

The civilization softens further as the Age of Affluence transitions into an Age of Intellect. Wealth is now available in such abundance that it far exceeds what is necessary "to supply the mere necessities, or even the luxuries of life," so excess funds are poured into advanced education and the pursuit of knowledge. This produces "surprising advances in natural science" and also in many other fields. But, says Glubb, the shadow side of this flourishing intellectual climate is such a luxuriance of "discussion, debate, and argument" that "public affairs drift from bad to worse, amid an unceasing cacophony of argument" that vitiates "the power of action."

In addition, except at the cutting edge, the quantitative increase in intellectual output tends to bring about a decline in quality. (As Gibbon famously remarked about Rome's Age of Intellect, "A crowd of critics, of compilers, of commentators, darkened the face of learning, and the decline of genius was soon followed by the corruption of taste."[5]) The excessively rational approach to life characteristic of the Age of Intellect also fosters "the unconscious growth of the idea that the human brain can solve the problems of the world" by mere cleverness, without effort, dedication, or sacrifice on the part of individuals. Thus problems are addressed with simplistic policies that are not supported by political will and are therefore doomed to failure.

However, the most dangerous byproduct of the unceasing cacophony is a growth in civil dissension. As Glubb notes, people are "interminably different, and intellectual arguments rarely lead to agreement." To the contrary, they lead to polarization, so "internal rivalries become more acute."

Another source of division within the polity arises from an influx of foreigners drawn irresistibly to the panoply of imperial wealth and glory. The result is an increasingly polyglot population that no longer shares the same values.[6] In fact, thanks to the demolition job performed by the intellectuals, the society is increasingly "value free"—that is, it no longer believes in much of anything or takes anything seriously. The original élan, the moral core, and the guiding ideal of the civilization are now a distant memory.

An Age of Decadence inevitably follows. Frivolity, aestheticism, hedonism, cynicism, pessimism, narcissism, consumerism, materialism, nihilism, fatalism, fanaticism, and other negative attributes, attitudes, and behaviors suffuse the population. Politics is increasingly corrupt, life increasingly unjust. A cabal of insiders accrues wealth and power at the expense of the citizenry, fostering a fatal opposition of interests between haves and have-nots. Mental and physical illness proliferates. The majority lives for bread and circuses; worships celebrities instead of divinities; takes its bearings from below rather than above; throws off social and moral restraints, especially on sexuality; shirks duties but insists on entitlements; and so forth.[7] The society's original vigor, virtue, and morale have been entirely effaced. Rotten to the core, the society awaits collapse, with only the date remaining to be determined.

In theory, says Glubb, a wider knowledge of this historical trend should enable societies to make different choices and thereby forestall the descent into decadence. In reality, however, he sees no escape from the socioeconomic dynamic he identifies. Stability and peace are bound to foster manufacture, trade, and the rise of a commercial class; affluence and all the later stages follow as a matter of course. And there is also no escape from the succession of generations; each new cohort grows up in altered circumstances that incline it to move further away from the original values, virtues, and ideals of the civilization. Rung by rung, the civilization drops ever lower on the ladder of decline.

Indeed, Glubb finds a remarkable regularity in the historical record. Barring an earlier dissolution due to external forces, it seems to take a mere ten generations for a civilization to traverse the arc from élan to decadence. Hence they appear to have a natural lifespan of roughly 250 years that human action can do little to extend.

The arc of decline described by Glubb is dissimilar only in detail and emphasis from that of most other writers. Spengler, for example, uses an organic metaphor to depict essentially the same process: a civilization that is born in spring, flourishes in summer, decays in autumn, dies in winter. Some, such as Toynbee, make practical failure (the topic of the next chapter), rather than moral decay, the crucial factor. Still others point to the growing divergence between elite and mass, between those at the top striving to uphold the civilization and an "internal proletariat" effectively bent on destroying it.[8] Thus Will and Ariel Durant note that, because political and economic expansion entails an increase in hierarchy and inequality,

> a society may find itself divided between a cultured minority and a majority of men and women too unfortunate by nature or circumstance to inherit or develop standards of excellence or taste. As this majority grows it acts as a cultural drag upon the minority; its ways of speech, dress, recreation, feeling, judgment, and thought spread upward [and cause] internal barbarization.[9]

In the end, therefore, even the elites are corrupted. There is no one left to defend a civilization that has grown oppressive, unjust, and frustrating.[10]

But these differences among the various authors are not important. For however they describe the process, or whatever causal factor they assert as most important, the terminus is always the same. The vital élan or inspiring ideal that impelled the society to greatness has been lost. What remains is decadence and barbarization.

But why are civilizations seemingly compelled to follow this path? After all, Spengler to the contrary notwithstanding, they are not organisms with a life of their own; they are created by human actions. So why can't they be made to last?

As noted previously, maintaining a civilization takes a continuous input of matter, energy, and morale, and the latter is actually the most important. What sustains a civilization is a strong commitment to its values, practices, and institutions—or, to put it another way, a firm belief in its moral and practical superiority. But commitment and belief are not immutable. On the contrary, they are bound to wither away.

We have already seen that matter and energy are governed by entropy—that is, they tend to travel downhill from a concentrated to a diffuse state (meaning that they are no longer useful or valuable for human purposes). But the trajectory described by Glubb and other authors suggests that the social order is also governed by a force that we can call moral entropy.[11] The original vigor and virtue of a civilization is morality in a highly concentrated form. As such, it has only one direction to travel: toward a less concentrated state.

In traditional societies governed by elders who incarnate and enforce the rule of custom, material conditions are relatively unchanging. Thus the same moral code tends to prevail for generation after generation. In civilizations, however, change is incessant. This exposes morals, mores, and morale to a continuous undertow of entropy. Hence the moral core of the society steadily erodes until vigor and virtue have been entirely displaced by decadence and decay.

In theory, moral reformation should be possible at any point along the way, thus forestalling the descent or even restoring the original élan. But it rarely happens in practice, and not only for the reasons given by Glubb.

First, until it terminates in decadence, the positive feedback loop seems to be a virtuous circle. Who can object to becoming wealthier and more powerful? Or to increasing social welfare and scientific knowledge? No one. Only "reactionaries" oppose "progress."

Second, as noted, the human mind is poor at foreseeing future consequences. So those living during the Age of Commerce will ignore the ecological exhaustion and thermodynamic losses that lurk in the future. Similarly, the proponents of the welfare state will not account for its long-term political, sociological, and psychological consequences. Nor will they understand that they may be foisting an unbearable fiscal burden on posterity. And propagandists for the Age of Intellect will not conceive that a society in which a million opinions bloom could foster faction instead of consensus and thereby render the society ungovernable.

For all these reasons, moral entropy tends to go unnoticed. Until the brute fact of decadence and decay imposes itself, the civilization seems to be on a grand march toward "greatness." The farsighted few who warn that progress is sowing the seeds of decline suffer the fate of Cassandra. And those who question the very notion of greatness—for instance, Rousseau, Thoreau, and Gandhi—are revered as great souls whose noble but eccentric ideas offer abundant food for thought but none for action. So the silent, stealthy erosion of the civilization's moral core proceeds unchecked. Once the damage is done, however, it is too late. Nothing is left but to suffer the consequences.

Nevertheless, we could possibly do a better job of managing or arresting decline if not for one final, fatal factor. Human beings are barely evolved primates driven by greed, fear, and other powerful emotions. Hence, said Edmund Burke, "History consists, for the greater part, of the miseries brought upon the world by pride, ambition, avarice, revenge, lust, sedition, hypocrisy, ungoverned zeal, and all the train of disorderly appetite."[12] In addition, humans are only partly rational, so they also suffer multiple mental aberrations—delusions, compulsions, manias, idées fixes, and the like. Indeed, as we have seen, the human mental and emotional constitution is better suited for hunting and gathering on the African savannah than for inhabiting a complex civilization.[13] At the pioneer stage of the cycle, when mores are strong and ideals compelling, the destructive aspects of human nature are kept in check. But as mores weaken and ideals fade, moral entropy works ever more powerfully to degrade the citizens.

In addition, moral entropy never acts alone to destroy morale. It is abetted and aggravated at every step along the way by the inability of rulers and ruled alike (but especially the former) to deal promptly and effectively with the challenges posed by increasing numbers and growing complexity. Let us therefore turn to the second way in which civilizations prepare their own demise: practical failure.

6
Practical Failure

> For civilization is not something inborn or imperishable; it must be acquired anew by every generation, and any serious interruption in its financing or its transmission may bring it to an end.
>
> Will Durant[1]

The most important reason why civilizations go from high morale and strong consensus to pessimism and division is moral entropy. But this is not the final answer. Of almost equal importance is the fact that those who direct the affairs of a mature civilization are engaged in a war against reality that they cannot win, because a series of insidious transformations has rendered the society dysfunctional and ungovernable. It lacks the ecological, social, financial, and intellectual capital required to solve its problems. Hence morale is gradually eroded, and discord increasingly fomented, by a succession of practical defeats.

As has been shown, a developing civilization grows steadily more complex and increasingly less manageable over time, preparing the way for its eventual demise. Only a race of supremely intelligent, rational, and wise beings could so order their affairs and so limit their behavior as to avoid this outcome. Human beings are not such a race. At best, they manage their affairs by muddling through—a mode of operation that has many virtues and advantages but that also postpones dealing with fundamental issues until they become intractable. At worst, they actively prepare their own downfall through greed, arrogance, obstinacy, shortsightedness, laziness, and stupidity.

Because humans are more focused on the present than the future, and complex systems are unpredictable, decisions at all levels of society are bound to be increasingly "suboptimal" as a civilization grows in complexity. In early times, when affairs are comparatively simple and morale is high, a united populace will tend to think and act with prudence, foresight, and due respect for the interests of posterity. (Witness the epigraph by John Adams in the previous chapter: the founding generation of Americans sacrificed so that their children and grandchildren could have a nobler life.) In later times, when affairs are far from simple and morale is low, the opposite is true. Selfishness crowds out sacrifice, the interests of mass and elite diverge, and the elite itself is divided into warring factions. Solvable problems turn into insolvable plights. Planning for the long term becomes an unaffordable luxury. The society drifts, following the line of least resistance by taking merely expedient actions that postpone rather than resolve problems. Posterity is left to fend for itself.

Complexity is only one part of the challenge. As it develops, a civilization accumulates an investment in physical and social infrastructure that increasingly limits its freedom of action, and it adheres to a certain way of thinking that increasingly limits its freedom of choice. These entrenched habits, patterns, structures, institutions, ideologies, and interests prevent adaptation to changed conditions.[2] In effect, civilizations suffer from a structural incapacity to respond to altered circumstances.

It could not be otherwise. Institutions are by their very nature resistant to change, for if not, society would be in a constant state of flux. As time goes on, institutions therefore grow steadily more hidebound, inflexible, and unresponsive. "Inertia in the scales of history weighs more heavily than change," said Barbara Tuchman.[3] With its ways of thinking and acting set in concrete, increasingly blind to reality and to alternative possibilities, an ossified civilization descends into a terminal stagnation that prepares its demise.

Like Gulliver, the civilization finds itself tied down by a multitude of vested interests—physical, social, economic, financial, political, and psychological. Enmeshed in this legacy of the past, it cannot save itself. Even if the will to change existed, it would take prodigious effort and many decades to overcome the legacy, but the will is lacking. The civilization's elites may understand that the system is dysfunctional, but fundamental reform would require major sacrifice on their part, so they fight to preserve their privilege and power instead. Increasingly polarized, they dissipate their energy in factional struggle instead of problem solving. Besides, says Ronald Wright, "They continue to prosper in darkening times long after the environment and general populace begin to suffer."[4] In the end, the elites prefer an advantageous present, however problematic, to an uncertain and possibly disadvantageous future. Again, the upshot is stagnation.

That being said, psychological vested interests are by far the greatest barriers to adaptation. "In general we find," said William Playfair, "that all nations are inclined to push to the extreme those means by which they have attained wealth and power; [in consequence] their ruin is thereby brought on with greater rapidity."[5]

Bluntly put, human societies are addicted to their ruling ideas and their received way of life, and they are fanatical in their defense. Hence they are extraordinarily reluctant to reform. "To admit error and cut losses," said Tuchman, "is rare among individuals, unknown among states."[6] Instead of changing their minds, leaders redouble their efforts to do what no longer works, wooden-headedly persisting in error until the bitter end.[7]

Even scientists, those supposedly rational beings, doggedly resist change when confronted with anomalies that call their theories into question.[8] Because scientific investigation is conducted in accordance with paradigms, any challenge to the old one threatens to render obsolete all the research produced under its aegis. Not unnaturally, the scientists who conducted that research do everything in their power to defend the old paradigm by arguing the anomalies away. In fact, new paradigms do not typically succeed purely on their merits but are championed by young Turks who take over the discipline by shoving aside old fogies. But the fogies are not entirely wrong in resisting change, says Thomas Kuhn: "retooling" is hard and is therefore "an extravagance to be reserved for the occasion that demands it."[9] Thus it almost always takes a genuine scientific crisis—anomalies so gross that they cannot be argued away—to create the space for a new paradigm.

If retooling is hard in the scientific sphere, how much more so in the social, economic, and political arena, where attachment to the old way of thinking and acting is far stronger and where much more is at stake than prestige. Discerning what is a genuine anomaly that calls into question the old order and what is a mere problem that can be solved with just a little more effort is also far from easy. Indeed, in the absence of a standard of truth similar to the scientific method, there are no clear criteria for deciding. Thus participants in the debate are, with rare exceptions, all partisan defenders of some vested interest or cherished ideology, however much they may couch their arguments in terms of the public interest.

Moreover, the debate takes place in an emotionally charged atmosphere. The society is in crisis. What used to work no longer does. Institutions and infrastructures have broken down. A hypertrophied bureaucracy strangles the society in red tape. Rent-seeking insiders batten on the public purse, and selfish elites feather their own nests. The gap separating rich and poor becomes a chasm. As problems multiply and become chronic, overloaded leaders struggle to cope. Addressing one problem creates new ones; not addressing small problems turns them into big ones. The elite is divided by interest or ideology into factions, so politics is gridlocked, or even fratricidal.[10] Mental health declines: there is increasing frustration, tension, division, disorder, and distress, so every form of irrationality flourishes. In the end, the social contract unravels. The populace and even members of the elite lose all faith in the system and in their leaders, who are seen as ineffective at best, incompetent and corrupt at worst.[11]

But if incompetent or corrupt leaders certainly make matters worse, they are not the real cause of failure. Faced with deteriorating ecological, physical, social, economic, and political conditions and with declining returns on the civilization's investment in complexity, even capable and honest leaders have no viable way forward. Although the problems may be insoluble, something must be done, and since expediency no longer suffices, they resort to stupidity—doing what has never worked in the past, what cannot succeed in the present, and what will destroy the future both morally and practically. First, by engaging in unnecessary wars or imperial ventures that drain the civilization of blood and treasure. Second, by buying off the populace with bread, circuses, and entitlements, thereby promising more than can be delivered over the long term. Third, by deliberately debasing the currency—that is, consciously adopting a policy of inflation.

The stupidity of the first should be self-evident: glory and booty notwithstanding, war is always physically, socially, and morally destructive. The stupidity of the second is that it will end in bankruptcy. But the stupidity of an inflationary policy requires amplification, for it is the most insidious.

Inflation is always an evasion of reality—an attempt to maintain an artificial prosperity that objective conditions would not otherwise allow.[12] Leaders resort to inflation because they are desperate. They have been backed into a corner by events and lack the moral courage or the political support to institute fundamental reforms, which would require them to inflict pain on the mass of commoners and vanquish powerful elites. (In addition, as previously noted, those in power instinctively understand that reforming a corrupt polity can precipitate chaos and collapse, so they legitimately fear embarking on change.) Charged with governing a populace accustomed to living well beyond its means, overwhelmed by a multiplicity of difficult problems, hemmed in by a host of vested interests, burdened by a deteriorating physical and social infrastructure that is increasingly costly to maintain, encumbered with ecological, thermodynamic, and fiscal debts that have come due, rulers bereft of backbone, ingenuity, and capital attempt to postpone the impending crisis by inflating, whether this takes the form of clipping coins, printing money, or loosening credit.

But it is a path to perdition. John Maynard Keynes described the peril in these words:

> By a continuing process of inflation, governments can confiscate, secretly and unobserved, an important part of the wealth of their citizens. By this method they not only confiscate, but they confiscate *arbitrarily*; and, while the process impoverishes many, it actually enriches some. The sight of this arbitrary rearrangement of riches strikes not only at security but at confidence in the equity of the existing distribution of wealth.... As the inflation proceeds... all permanent relations between debtors and creditors, which form the ultimate foundation of capitalism, become so utterly disordered

as to be almost meaningless; and the process of wealth-getting degenerates into a gamble and a lottery.[13]

Hence, Keynes concluded, "There is no subtler, no surer means of overturning the existing basis of society than to debauch the currency. The process engages all the hidden forces of economic law on the side of destruction, and does it in a manner which not one man in a million is able to diagnose."[14]

In essence, inflation punishes prudence and thrift, while rewarding their opposites.[15] By favoring vice over virtue, it imperils not only the ultimate foundation of a capitalist economy, as Keynes says, but it also corrodes the moral basis of civil society. For once people realize that their wealth is being secretly and arbitrarily confiscated and their welfare systematically degraded by underhanded rulers, then the social contract is broken, with possible revolutionary consequences.[16]

Describing the situation in Weimar Germany, Otto Friedrich epitomizes the devastating demoralization caused by serious inflation:

> The fundamental quality of the disaster was a complete loss of faith in the functioning of society. Money is important not just as a medium of exchange, after all, but as a standard by which society judges our work, and thus ourselves. If all money becomes worthless, then so does all government, and all society, and all standards. In the madness of 1923, a workman's work was worthless, a widow's savings were worthless, everything was worthless.[17]

That inflation is demoralizing should come as no surprise. After all, *sound money* is practically synonymous with prudence, probity, self-restraint, and foresight—that is, all the political virtues needed for a civilization's long-term vitality and viability. Unsound money is bound to produce the contrary.[18]

It may be objected that there can be no harm in just a little bit of inflation if that is what it takes to grease the wheels of commerce and foster economic growth. But this is a fatal delusion. Those who propose the policy and carry it out are convinced that they know how to tame the tiger they are unleashing, that they are in control of events. Once past a certain point, however, when the society has become so overextended that inflation is a desperate last resort, the delusion of control is revealed to be what it was all along: hubris.

First, recall the discussion of exponential growth. At the relatively low inflation rate of 3.6 percent, the value of a dollar is halved in twenty years (and annihilated in one hundred). Second, as Keynes says, even at such a low rate, an inflationary policy is still a secret and arbitrary confiscation. Third, it is insidious, because "not one man in a million" can spot the swindle. Fourth, inflation is addictive: when a little bit does not suffice, the temptation is to prescribe more of the same, which puts the society on a slippery slope from which it may never recover. Finally, a deliberate policy of inflation is tantamount to an abdication of responsibility and an admission of failure on the part of the governing class. It demonstrates that they have allowed the society's problems to become intractable and lack the competence or the integrity to deal with them. No matter how modest or benign it may seem at first, an inflationary policy is therefore always suicidal in the long run. It has been tried many times and has always failed. It does not solve the problems of the society; it aggravates them and leads inexorably on toward self-destruction.

Inflation is not, of course, the most monumental stupidity of which human beings are capable—war is more immediately and directly destructive to civilized life—but it best illustrates what happens when a civilization reaches an impasse. With no good options left, leaders can only choose what seems to be the least bad policy in the short term, even though it is self-destructive in the long term.

Tainter describes the predicament of the Roman Empire:

> Most actions that the Roman government took in response to crises—such as debasing the currency, raising taxes, expanding the army, and conscripting labor—were practical solutions to immediate problems. It would have been unthinkable not to adopt such measures. Cumulatively, however, these practical steps made the empire ever weaker, as the capital stock (agricultural land and peasants) was depleted through conscription and taxation.[19]

In the end, says Tainter, "The empire could no longer afford the problem of its own existence."[20]

A mature civilization is caught in an entropy trap from which escape is well nigh impossible. Because the available energy and resources can no longer maintain the existing level of complexity, the civilization begins to consume itself by borrowing from the future and feeding off the past, thereby preparing the way for an eventual implosion. As Homer-Dixon puts it, Rome "literally burn[ed] through its capital" in increasingly desperate efforts to stave off collapse.[21]

Once a civilization has reached this point, not even a miraculous new technology can save it. Even if it had the will, it no longer has either the resources or the time to dismantle the legacy of the past and build the infrastructure of a viable future. This is the tragedy of civilization: its very "greatness"—its panoply of wealth and power—turns against it and brings it down.

Reform and revival are not inconceivable, only extraordinarily difficult and costly.[22] Ataturk's foundation of modern Turkey on the ruins of the Ottoman Empire and the success of the Meiji Reformation in Japan show what can be done with vision and leadership. But fundamental reform always involves "creative destruction," as both the Turkish and Japanese cases illustrate. Ataturk had to overthrow the Ottoman sultanate and also fight a war of independence against occupying armies that unleashed extensive "collateral damage" on Greeks and Armenians, not to mention the Turks themselves. Similarly, the Meiji Restoration entailed a civil war lasting three years. But these cases were exceptions that prove the rule: "Sadly," says Homer-Dixon, "history shows that most human civilizations overextend the growth phase of their adaptive cycle, so they eventually suffer deep collapse."[23]

Why reform is both difficult and perilous was elucidated by Machiavelli:

> There is nothing more difficult to carry out, nor more doubtful of success, nor more dangerous to handle, than to initiate a new order of things. For the reformer has enemies in all those who profit by the old order, and only lukewarm defenders in all those who would profit by the new order, this lukewarmness arising partly from fear of their adversaries, who have the laws in their favour; and partly from the incredulity of mankind, who do not truly believe in anything new until they have had actual experience of it.[24]

Not surprisingly, fundamental reform is undertaken only as a last resort, when conditions are already so dire that there is nothing left to lose.

All that remains is to underscore the grim alliance of moral entropy and practical failure. Fatal alone, lethal together, they conspire to bring down a civilization whose growth has exceeded the limits of what is physically possible and whose development has engendered a complex nexus of social, economic, fiscal, and political problems with no feasible solutions. At some point the "stupendous fabric [yields] to the pressure of its own weight," and the civilization collapses.

Conclusion
Trampled Down, Barren, and Bare

> Wealth and power have never been long permanent in any place....
> [T]hey travel over the face of the earth, something like a caravan of merchants. On their arrival everything is found green and fresh; while they remain, all is bustle and abundance, and, when gone, all is left trampled down, barren, and bare.
>
> William Playfair[1]

Civilizations are unnatural accumulations of wealth and power that cannot be sustained over the long term. Insuperable biophysical limits combine with innate human fallibility to precipitate eventual collapse. Any one of the factors discussed above would suffice to sicken a civilization. All of them together are lethal, because each exacerbates the rest. Decline and fall are therefore "overdetermined"—that is, the product of a multiplicity of causes tending toward the same effect. As Gibbon said, instead of asking why Rome fell, "we should rather be surprised that it had subsisted so long."[2]

Reducing the process to its essence, a civilization declines when it has exhausted its physical and moral capital. A civilization begins with abundant resources, inspiring ideals, strong morals, solvable problems, and high morale. "Green and fresh," it accumulates wealth and power. However, its rise to dominance also prepares its downfall, for although greatness brings "bustle and abundance," it also entails scarce resources, faded ideals, loose morals, intractable problems, and, in consequence, lost morale. In addition, because "the general tendency of wealth and power is to enervate a people, to make them proud and indolent," they succumb to hubris and become the authors of their own demise.[3] Every civilization therefore ends "all…trampled, down, barren, and bare."

It will not have escaped the reader's attention that the signs and symptoms of impending collapse roughly sketched above are pervasive.[4] Ecological problems, exponential pressures, thermodynamic losses, risky complexity, moral decay, and human incapacity are evident everywhere, differing only in extent and degree among the various regions and societies that make up modern industrial civilization.[5]

Moreover, all these societies are now interconnected in a vast and complex world system far beyond anyone's ken or control. We therefore confront a potential worldwide collapse, as a cascade of failure brings down a global order that is now approximately 250 years old (i.e., close to what Glubb deems to be the natural lifespan of a civilization).[6] Having built up a "stupendous fabric" far beyond anything that Gibbon could have conceived, the implosion to come seems destined to be equally stupendous.

Before civilization became universal, the consequences of decline and fall may have been catastrophic for a particular society and for many or even most of its inhabitants, but they were not fatal to civilization itself. There were always others to keep the flame alive. Or a lurking horde of barbarians poised to bring fresh blood to a tired and moribund society. But now that a highly interdependent, global, industrial civilization extends its monopoly to the ends of the earth, there are no others to pick up the baton, nor any barbarian reservoirs to replenish its élan. "Collapse, if and when it comes again, will this time be global," says Tainter.[7]

It will also be uniquely devastating. Given the enormous growth of populations and the extent of ecological devastation and social dislocation caused by industrialization—as well as the degree to which the methods and materials of traditional agriculture have been abandoned in the rush to ramp up yields by converting fossil fuel into food—a gradual and gentle transition to a viable agrarian civilization capable of supporting large numbers of people and a reasonable level of complexity is extremely unlikely. In fact, says Tainter, the collapse of today's highly developed societies "would almost certainly entail vast disruptions and overwhelming loss of life, not mention a significantly lower standard of living for the survivors."[8] Wright's metaphor perfectly captures our plight: "As we climbed the ladder of progress, we kicked out the rungs below," leaving ourselves with no non-catastrophic way back to a less complex mode of existence.[9]

At this point, even a return to hunting and gathering would be challenging. Apart from a few bands of isolated Tupi-Guarani in the Amazon, almost all of the remaining, scattered tribal peoples have lost the territory, knowledge, and traditions that would enable them to survive if industrial civilization were to collapse.[10]

What is to be done? First, we must recognize that the deep structural problems elucidated above have no feasible solutions. Like Glubb, but for different reasons, Tainter does not believe that today's societies can escape the dynamic that eventuates in collapse. A military-industrial arms race among the sub-units of the existing global civilization "drives increased complexity and resource consumption regardless of costs, human or ecological."[11]

Hence, second, the task is not to forestall a foreordained collapse but, rather, to salvage as much as possible from it, lest the fall precipitate a dark age in which the arts and adornments of civilization are partially or completely lost.

To this end, just as prudent mariners carry lifeboats and practice abandoning ship, a global civilization in its terminal phase would be well advised to prepare arks, storehouses, and banks designed to preserve the persons, tools, and materials with which to retain or reconstitute some semblance of civilized life post-collapse.[12]

This appeal to prudence will not be readily accepted. For the hubris of every civilization is that it is, like the Titanic, unsinkable. Hence the motivation to plan for shipwreck is lacking. In addition, the civilization's contradictions and difficulties are seen not as symptoms of impending collapse but, rather, as problems to be solved by better policies and personnel. In other words, the populace does not yet understand that the civilization has reached an impasse. As Tainter notes, "It takes protracted hardship to convince people that the world to which they have been accustomed has changed irrevocably."[13]

Moreover, although collapse may be foreordained, its course and timing are largely unpredictable. Collapse could happen suddenly or gradually, sooner or later, so why act now? To make matters worse, preparing for this uncertain future requires present sacrifice—that is, the diversion of resources from both current consumption and from the task of coping with today's problems—at a time when those very same resources are becoming scarcer and more expensive. In short, denial, evasion, and procrastination are all but inevitable.[14]

Thus if preparations for collapse are made at all, they are likely to be too little and too late. Modern civilization is therefore bound for a worse fate than the Titanic. When it sinks, the lifeboats, if any, will be ill provisioned, and no one will come to its rescue. Humanity will undoubtedly survive. Civilization as we know it will not.

Although it would be intellectually dishonest of me to suggest any other outcome—a tragic denouement followed by a lengthy time of troubles—I can envision an alternative to civilization as it is currently conceived and constituted. This alternative, which could not be imposed but would have to emerge slowly and organically, should allow humanity to thrive in reasonable numbers on a limited planet for millennia to come. But it would require a fundamental change in the ethos of civilization—to wit, the deliberate renunciation of greatness in favor of simplicity, frugality, and fraternity.[15] For the pursuit of greatness is always a manifestation of hubris, and hubris is always punished by nemesis. Whether human beings are capable of such sagacity and self-restraint is a question only the future can answer.

Bibliographic Note

The literature on decline and fall is vast, and the number of works relevant to the many topics discussed above borders on the infinite, so the list of sources is necessarily selective. I will let those sources speak mostly for themselves and use this space to indicate a few works that might interest and enlighten readers primarily concerned about the plight of our own civilization.

Will and Ariel Durant's *The Lessons of History* is succinct, readable, and wise; no better guide to the enduring truths of the historical process can be imagined. However, Ian Morris's *Why the West Rules—For Now* speaks more directly to our current condition. The topical title does not do justice to this magnificent one-volume history of the human race from its earliest origins to the current geopolitical moment. Morris shows how a dynamic interplay of human nature, geography, and technology has repeatedly fostered "social development"—that is, civilized complexity—along with the "paradoxes of development" that work to degrade or destroy that complexity. He concludes his sweeping survey by disclosing the depth of our current crisis. As has happened numerous times in human history, increased population, consumption, and complexity have pushed our civilization up against a developmental "hard ceiling." Given the impossibility of simply extrapolating current trends—imagine gargantuan cities of 150 million!—humanity must now either break through that ceiling to achieve "Singularity," an unprecedented mastery of the historical process, or face a sudden collapse into "Nightfall." In other words, according to Morris, the choice before humankind is utopia or oblivion, and achieving utopia will require a quasi-miraculous transformation of human culture, if not human nature.

John Michael Greer's assessment of our predicament is only slightly less stark. He agrees with Morris that we have hit a hard ceiling, but he does not believe that oblivion is the sole alternative to an unattainable utopia. In *The Long Descent*, Greer argues instead that we will experience a more gradual (but still quite traumatic) "catabolic" collapse. Periods of crisis and stability will alternate as human societies descend a bumpy staircase of declining population, consumption, and complexity. Future generations will feed off the corpse of industrial civilization until the bones have been picked clean and humanity subsists once again on nothing but solar energy. However, this need not entail a hand-to-mouth existence. He envisions a relatively rich agrarian economy resembling that of Tokugawa Japan. (Compare my vision of "Bali with electronics" and "wiser savagery" in *Plato's Revenge* [Cambridge, MA: MIT Press, 2011], 167–193.) In *The Ecotechnic Future*, Greer describes the successive stages of this jarring descent in more detail and urges practical steps that will both ease the passage and accomplish his vision. Finally, his *The Wealth of Nature* puts forward a theory of "economics as if survival mattered."

Thomas Homer-Dixon's *The Upside of Down* combines anecdotes, interviews, and observations with analysis to provide a rich and detailed portrait of the hard ceiling. While not minimizing the risk of "deep collapse," Homer-Dixon tries to cast the impending breakdown in a positive light—it could inspire "a burst of creativity, reorganization, and renewal," he says [269]. But he emphasizes that nothing can preserve our profligate and arrogant way of life. Posterity will have to live in more resilient societies that respect natural limits and govern themselves accordingly.

Joseph A. Tainter's *The Collapse of Complex Societies* sets forth his pioneering theory of declining returns on the human investment in complexity. To understand the world in Tainter's terms is to inhabit a transformed reality—one in which many of our most vaunted achievements, such as higher education or technological medicine, are now seen as costly mixed blessings. Highly influential, the book deserves the overused epithet seminal for having inspired or informed later work on decline, resilience, net energy, EROI, and the like. Unfortunately, Tainter tends to downplay or even dismiss alternative explanations for collapse. I argue to the contrary that no single factor can account for the demise of civilizations, which is brought about by many causes that aggregate into an intractable problematique greater by far than the mere sum of the causes.

David Hackett Fischer's *The Great Wave* is a study of inflationary episodes in history. It illuminates our current predicament by showing that what we are living through today has occurred many times in the past. As populations and economies grow, demand for goods outstrips supply. Elites seeking to preserve their status and wealth typically respond to emerging scarcity with inflationary policies that make matters worse. The result is social conflict or even revolution—a time of troubles that lasts until a new political and economic equilibrium is established.

Jack A. Goldstone's *Revolution and Rebellion in the Early Modern World* complements and amplifies Fischer by showing how popular grievances, fiscal crises, factional infighting, and elite disaffection prepare the ground for eventual revolution by exposing the state as unjust and ineffective.

To make sense of today's reality, a basic grasp of systems, complexity, and chaos is indispensable. With regard to systems, Donella H. Meadows's *Thinking in Systems* is an excellent primer. *Limits to Growth*, the famous study that Meadows and her colleagues prepared for the Club of Rome in 1972, demonstrated the utility of applied systems thought for understanding the world dynamically. The study (updated in 2004) is even more relevant to the problematique of industrial civilization today than when it first appeared. (In retrospect, it seems clear that the most vociferous critics of the original simply did not deign to understand the logic of the model before dismissing it as flawed and foolish.) Melanie Mitchell's *Complexity* is a concise and readable exposition of a challenging topic; Scott E. Page's *Understanding Complexity* conveys the same basic information in lecture form. John H. Miller and Scott E. Page's *Complex Adaptive Systems* is more challenging but still accessible and offers an abundance of real-world examples. John Gribbin's *Deep Simplicity* is a short and readable introduction to chaos, and Nassim Nicholas Taleb's *The Black Swan* warns of the hidden, unforeseeable dangers that lurk in chaotic systems.

When societies collapse, they often go temporarily insane. Gustave Le Bon's *The Crowd* is a classic treatment of what happens when people mob together to form a crowd driven by irrational impulses. For one concrete instance of mass insanity, see Simon Schama's *Citizens*, a gripping account of the French Revolution.

There are many critics of civilization in general and of modern industrial civilization in particular, and I have included a representative selection in the list of sources. To single out just a few, the finest anthropological critique remains Claude Lévi-Strauss's *Tristes Tropiques*, and the best psychological critique is still Sigmund Freud's *Civilization and Its Discontents*. Both reveal how difficult and painful it is for people to live in complex civilizations that frustrate basic human needs. F. A. Hayek's *The Road to Serfdom* shows how increased complexity inevitably magnifies the role of the state, drives up costs, lowers efficiency, and deprives individuals of personal autonomy. Along the same lines, my own *Plato's Revenge* criticizes the amoral destructiveness of Hobbesian political economy and proposes a Platonic alternative. For something less academic than all of the above, Ronald Wright's *A Short History of Progress* is not only short, but also sardonic and amusing.

Finally, literature has some light to cast on the subject. Pablo Neruda's *The Heights of Macchu Picchu* pays homage to the countless unnamed beings whose sacrificial blood and bone built the ancient cities. In *Ishmael*, Daniel Quinn records a wise gorilla's sly critique of agricultural civilization. Gabriel García Márquez's acclaimed *One Hundred Years of Solitude* recounts the rise and fall of little Macondo, a place out of time where magic and reality intertwine. Macondo's journey from dawn to decadence exemplifies the pitiless arc of civilization: one day we, too, will be "one with Nineveh and Tyre."

Notes

[1] Edward Gibbon, *The History of the Decline and Fall of the Roman Empire*, ed. and abridged David P. Womersley (New York, NY: Penguin, 2001), 435.

Preface

[1] I define *civilization* in accordance with *The American Heritage Dictionary of the English Language* (1975): "1. A condition of human society marked by an advanced stage of development in the arts and sciences and by corresponding social, political, and cultural complexity." This broad definition makes empires part of, but not necessarily synonymous with, civilizations. However, the semantic distinction is not critical, because (as will be seen) the same dynamic applies to both.

[2] For example, Thomas Homer-Dixon, *The Upside of Down* (Washington, DC: Island Press, 2006). See also Ian Morris, *Why the West Rules—For Now* (New York, NY: Farrar, Straus and Giroux, 2010), 557–622.

[3] William Ophuls, *Plato's Revenge* (Cambridge, MA: MIT Press, 2011).

[4] Wendell Berry, *The Unsettling of America* (San Francisco, CA: Sierra Club Books, 1977), 131.

Introduction

[1] Discourses on the First Ten Books of Titus Livius, III, xliii, in Niccolò Machiavelli, *The Historical, Political, and Diplomatic Writings*, vol. 2, trans. Christian E. Detmold (Boston, MA: J. R. Osgood, 1882), 422.

[2] Herman Kahn et al., *The Next 200 Years* (New York, NY: Morrow, 1976), 1.

[3] Democratic institutions, to the extent that they encourage a people to demand more of the polity than can reasonably be supplied over the

long term, exacerbate almost all the problems described below. Mass democracy is also in large part a sham. To be meaningful, democracy requires settings that allow direct knowledge of persons and issues. See William Ophuls, *Plato's Revenge* (Cambridge, MA: MIT Press, 2011), 136–137, 139, 143–144, 147, 149–150. What is worse, mass democracy is liable to mass madness. See Gustave Le Bon, *The Crowd* (Mineola, NY: Dover, 2002).

[4] In one sense, civilizations are incomparable. As chaotic systems that start from different initial conditions, they necessarily differ markedly in what they become. Thus facile comparisons should be resisted. See, for instance, Vaclav Smil, *Why America Is Not a New Rome* (Cambridge, MA: MIT Press, 2010). Nevertheless, just as each human being is unique, yet exhibits roughly similar propensities and goes through similar stages of life, once we abstract from the singularities we shall find that civilizations too have important features in common and follow a similar trajectory. This book isolates those features and identifies that trajectory.

[5] See Joseph A. Tainter, *The Collapse of Complex Societies* (Cambridge, England: Cambridge University Press, 1988), 70, 87, 151–152, 202–203.

[6] Will and Ariel Durant, *The Lessons of History* (New York, NY: Simon & Schuster, 1968), 88.

[7] My translation of *Devuélvame el esclavo que enterraste* from Pablo Neruda, *The Heights of Macchu Picchu*, bilingual edition, trans. Nathaniel Tarn (New York, NY: Farrar, Straus and Giroux, 1966), 58.

[8] Gibbon, op. cit., 743.

[9] Civilizations are like pyramid schemes that are viable only while growing, says Ronald Wright in *A Short History of Progress* (New York, NY: Carroll & Graf, 2005), 83–84. Similarly, Ian Morris in *Why the West Rules—For Now* (New York, NY: Farrar, Straus and Giroux, 2010), 560, says that civilizations rarely hit a "developmental ceiling" and then stagnate; they either break through or collapse.

[10] Cited Guglielmo Ferrero, *Characters and Events of Roman History* (New York, NY: Barnes & Noble, 2005), 2.

[11] Will Durant, *Caesar and Christ: The Story of Civilization*, vol. 3 (New York, NY: Simon & Schuster, 1944), 665. See also Gibbon, op. cit., 427–428: it was "the loss of freedom, of virtue, and of honour," not the barbarian invasions, that doomed the empire of the West. In addition, see Arnold J. Toynbee, *A Study of History*, Vol. 1: Abridgement of Volumes I–VI by D. C. Somervell (New York, NY: Oxford University Press, 1987), 273, for one instance of his oft-reiterated conclusion that the death of a great civilization is almost always a suicide.

Chapter 1

[1] Seneca, *Morals*, ed. Roger L'Estrange, 6th Amer. ed. (Philadelphia, PA: Grigg & Elliot, 1834), 134.

[2] Cited anon., "Perceptions of Forests," *Unasylva* no. 213 (Rome, Italy: FAO, 2003), 1.

[3] For the purposes of my argument, I shall define *complexity* as greater economic, social, and political scale, institutionalization, specialization, differentiation, and stratification. Thus a city is more complex than a village, because it is not only larger but also has more roles, a greater division of labor, finer gradations of class, a more elaborate hierarchy, and so forth. For more extended definitions, see Joseph A. Tainter, *The Collapse of Complex Societies* (Cambridge, England: Cambridge University Press, 1988), 4, and Patricia Crone, *Pre-Industrial Societies* (Oxford, England: Oneworld, 2003), 1–10. When I use the word in another sense—for instance, as an attribute of complex adaptive systems—it will be obvious from the context.

[4] See Clive Ponting, *A Green History of the World*, rev. and updated (New York, NY: Penguin, 2007), as well as the many references therein. See also J. Donald Hughes, *Pan's Travail* (Baltimore, MD: Johns Hopkins University Press, 1996), and George Perkins Marsh, *Man and Nature*

(New York, NY: General Books, 2009 [1864]), which recounted the same sorry tale almost a century and a half earlier.

5. David R. Montgomery, *Dirt* (Berkeley, CA: University of California Press, 2008); William F. Ruddiman, *Plows, Plagues, and Petroleum* (Princeton, NJ: Princeton University Press, 2007); Vernon Gill Carter and Tom Dale, *Topsoil and Civilization*, rev. ed. (Norman, OK: University of Oklahoma Press, 1975). The human consequences of adopting agriculture as a mode of production were also considerable. See Jared Diamond, "The Worst Mistake in the History of the Human Race," *Discover* (May 1987), 64–66, for a provocative summary, and Daniel Quinn, *The Story of B* (New York, NY: Bantam, 1997), 258–275 for an even more provocative timeline of the social "distress" caused by the introduction and further development of agriculture. The fateful political consequences of adopting the agricultural mode of production are the topic of Jean-Jacques Rousseau's famous "Discourse on the Origin and Foundations of Inequality" in *The First and Second Discourses*, ed. Roger D. Masters and trans. Judith R. Masters (New York, NY: St. Martin's, 1964).

6. Crone, op. cit., 9. See also Rousseau, op. cit.

7. I define *collapse* as a rapid, significant loss of complexity (for which see n. 3 above) such that the society becomes markedly simpler and less able to accomplish what was previously within its powers. At a minimum, it loses its "greatness." (Compare Tainter, op. cit., 4–5.) The post-Soviet state of Russia provides a concrete image of the dysfunction, demoralization, and distress that can follow in the wake of collapse. When the center no longer holds, William Butler Yeats's "mere anarchy" is loosed, with dire consequences. At an extreme, the society becomes "one with Nineveh and Tyre."

8. Paul Kennedy, *The Rise and Fall of the Great Powers* (New York, NY: Vintage, 1989).

9. Steven Solomon, *Water* (New York, NY: Harper, 2010).

[10] Replacing natural forests with artificial ones is not a solution: the latter are simplified, impoverished, anti-ecological counterfeits of the real thing. See Bernd Heinrich, "Clear-Cutting the Truth About Trees," *The New York Times*, December 20, 2009.

[11] Donella Meadows et al., *Limits to Growth: The 30-Year Update* (White River Junction, VT: Chelsea Green, 2004), 137, 162–167, and William R. Catton, *Overshoot* (Champaign, IL: Illini Books, 1982). See also Mathis Wackernagel and William Rees, *Our Ecological Footprint* (Gabriola Island, BC: New Society, 1996), for an exceptionally useful and graphic way of conceiving and quantifying overshoot.

Chapter 2

[1] Transcript of "Arithmetic, Population and Energy," *Global Public Media*, August 29, 2004. See also Albert A. Bartlett et al., *The Essential Exponential* (Lincoln, NE: University of Nebraska Center for Science, Mathematics & Computer Education, 2004), a collection of essays, mostly quite technical, on all aspects of exponential growth.

[2] Donella Meadows et al., *Limits to Growth: The 30-Year Update* (White River Junction, VT: Chelsea Green, 2004), 19, emphasis in original. See also the rest of the chapter for graphic illustrations of exponential growth.

[3] This fact does not depend on the rate of growth, which controls *when* the doubling occurs, but not the quantity.

[4] I have adapted this example from Bartlett's lecture.

[5] Among other things, there may be limits to innovation. See Thomas Homer-Dixon, *The Ingenuity Gap* (New York, NY: Vintage, 2002); Tyler Cohen, *The Great Stagnation* (Seattle WA: Amazon Kindle, 2011); James A. Brander, "Presidential Address: Innovation in retrospect and prospect," *Canadian Journal of Economics* 43, no. 4 (November 2010), 1087–1121; Peter Thiel, "The End of the Future," *National Review*, October 3, 2011.

6. For a fuller explanation of the shortcomings of the human mind in relation to civilization, see William Ophuls, *Plato's Revenge* (Cambridge, MA: MIT Press, 2011), 51–52, 70–77.
7. Discounting the future is not the sole problem. The sunk costs (and vested interests) of an infrastructure predicated on fossil fuels also make it difficult, costly, and painful to change.

Chapter 3
1. *The Nature of the Physical World* (Whitefish, MT: Kessinger, 2005), 74.
2. Ecological exhaustion and entropic loss are intimately related. When a rainforest is cut down, the ecologist focuses on the loss of habitat, the effects on climate, the extinction of species, and so on—that is, damage to the integrity of ecosystems. Whereas the physicist focuses on the downhill movement of energy from useful to useless. The vast energy potential of the living forest has been depleted, so entropy has increased. They are, therefore, complementary ways of accounting for the harm done to pre-existing natural systems by human action.
3. F. H. King, *Farmers of Forty Centuries* (Mineola, NY: Dover, 2004).
4. David Pimentel and Marcia H. Pimentel, *Food, Energy, and Society*, 3rd ed. (Boca Raton, FL: CRC Press. 2007).
5. Thomas Homer-Dixon, *The Upside of Down* (Washington, DC: Island Press, 2006), 85–94. See also Charles A. S. Hall and John W. Day, Jr., "Revisiting the Limits to Growth After Peak Oil," *American Scientist* 97 (May/June 2009), 230–237; Charles A. S. Hall et al., "Peak Oil, EROI, Investments and the Economy in an Uncertain Future" in David Pimentel, ed. *Biofuels, Solar and Wind as Renewable Energy Systems* (New York: Springer, 2008), 109–132; Charles A. S. Hall et al., "What Is the Minimum EROI That a Sustainable Society Must Have?" *Energies* 2, no. 1 (2009): 25–47, which suggests that three to one is the absolute minimum.

6 One of the largest recent discoveries is the Sugar Loaf field, a super elephant in deep water off the coast of Brazil. It is estimated to contain thirty-three billion barrels of oil equivalent. ["The next oil giant?" *The Economist*, May 19, 2007. See also "Filling up the future," *The Economist*, November 5, 2011.] Current world consumption is approximately ninety million barrels a day. Provided it can be fully exploited—the geological and technical challenges are enormous—Sugarloaf would therefore satisfy world demand for one year.

Chapter 4

1 Paul Ormerod, *Why Most Things Fail* (New York, NY: Wiley, 2007), 221.
2 Donella H. Meadows, *Thinking in Systems*, ed. Diana Wright (White River Junction, VT: Chelsea Green, 2008), 167–168.
3 Joseph A. Tainter, *The Collapse of Complex Societies* (Cambridge, England: Cambridge University Press, 1988), 23, citing Randell H. McGuire. See also idem, "Complexity, Problem Solving, and Sustainable Societies," in Robert Costanza et al., eds. *Getting Down to Earth* (Washington, DC: Island Press, 1996), 61–76.
4 Thomas Homer-Dixon, *The Ingenuity Gap* (New York, NY: Vintage, 2002).
5 Joseph A. Tainter, "Human Resource Use: Timing and Implications for Sustainability," paper delivered to 94th Annual Meeting of the Ecological Society of America (2009): 2 (archived at www.oildrum.com/node/6942).
6 Tainter, "Complexity," 62.
7 Ibid., 66.
8 For instance, the US has about 85,000 dams of which more than 4,400 are considered susceptible to failure, with potentially catastrophic consequences in some cases. However, the cost of repair would be staggering, and fixing them would not increase the productive capacity of the country but simply maintain the status quo. [See Henry

Fountain, "Danger Pent Up Behind Aging Dams," *The New York Times*, February 21, 2011.] Unfortunately, the same is true of American infrastructure across the board. Most of the nation's bridges, highways, airports, and ports are old or obsolete and need expensive maintenance or upgrading just to remain operational.

[9] Tyler Cowen, *The Great Stagnation* (Seattle, WA: Amazon Kindle, 2011). See also William Ophuls, *Requiem for Modern Politics* (Boulder, CO: Westview Press, 1997), 160–168.

[10] Tainter provides numerous other examples in *Collapse*, 91–126.

[11] C. Northcote Parkinson, *Parkinson's Law* (New York, NY: Ballantine, 1987). See also F. A. Hayek, *The Road to Serfdom*, ed. Bruce Caldwell (Chicago, IL: University of Chicago Press, 2007), and Alexander J. Motyl, *Imperial Ends* (New York, NY: Columbia University Press, 2001), 39–40.

[12] Per Bak, *How Nature Works* (New York, NY: Springer, 1999), 105. See also John H. Miller and Scott E. Page, *Complex Adaptive Systems* (Princeton, NJ: Princeton University Press, 2007), 65–77, for a discussion of how greater interconnectedness and interdependence produce "self-organized criticality."

[13] Scott E. Page, *Understanding Complexity* (Chantilly, VA: The Teaching Company, 2009), lecture 12.

[14] Meadows, op. cit., 100.

[15] Charles P. Kindleberger, et al., *Manias, Panics, and Crashes*, 5th ed. (New York, NY: Wiley, 2005); Carmen M. Reinhart and Kenneth Rogoff, *This Time Is Different* (Princeton, NJ: Princeton University Press, 2009).

[16] Meadows, op. cit., 145, citing Jay Forrester, emphasis in original.

[17] Donella H. Meadows, "Systems Dynamics Meets the Press," *In Context* (Autumn 1989), 16–21. See also Victor Davis Hanson, *Fields Without Dreams* (New York, NY: Free Press, 1997), a passionate defense of the agrarian way of life as socially and economically essential for a healthy polity.

[18] Meadows devotes a whole chapter of *Thinking in Systems* to describing these traps: 111–141.

[19] Ibid., 146; Jared Diamond, *Collapse* (New York, NY: Penguin, 2006), 79–119, 419–440.

[20] Thomas Homer-Dixon, *The Upside of Down* (Washington, DC: Island Press, 2006), 16 (and see also 253–254, 281–287).

[21] Will Durant, *The Reformation: The Story of Civilization*, vol. 6 (New York, NY: Simon & Schuster, 1957), 190.

[22] Niall Ferguson, "Complexity and Collapse: Empires on the Edge of Chaos," *Foreign Affairs* 89, no. 2 (March/April 2010), 18–32 at 32. Along the same lines, but arguing from different premises, see W. R. Connor, "Why Were We Surprised?" *American Scholar* 60, no. 2 (Spring 1991), 175–184.

[23] See Simon Schama, *Citizens* (New York, NY: Vintage, 1990). When the credit needed to keep the ship of state afloat dried up, the king, having exhausted all possible administrative remedies, had no choice but to throw open the door to political change. It was only then that other factors came into play—food shortages and other long-standing grievances, resentment of *les grands* and popular hatred of the queen, the spread of a populist ideology derived from Rousseau's *Contrat Social*, the example of the American Revolution, free-floating anger and paranoia, and more. Together these virtually guaranteed that what came through the door would be a terrible, bloody revolution instead of a controlled and gradual transition to constitutional monarchy.

[24] Gustave Le Bon, *The Crowd* (Mineola, NY: Dover, 2002).

Chapter 5

[1] Letter to Abigail Adams, post 12 May 1780, archived at www.masshist.org/digitaladams/aea/cfm/doc.cfm?id=L17800512jasecond, spelling corrected.

[2] A soldier's soldier, Glubb was for many years the commanding general of Jordan's Arab Legion. However, he was also an amateur historian of some repute, and toward the end of his life, he set forth his theory of historical cycles in an essay entitled "The Fate of Empires." Based on his study of eleven empires from ancient Assyria and Persia to modern Russia and Britain, it was first published in *Blackwood's Magazine* in December 1976 and later reprinted in Sir John Glubb, *The Fate of Empires and Search for Survival* (Edinburgh, Scotland: William Blackwood, 1978), 1–28. For the sake of clarity, continuity, and completeness, I have amplified and extended his argument at one or two places. Given the brevity of the essay, I have not thought it necessary to link each quote to a specific page.

[3] Although Glubb does not mention Ibn Khaldun, he seems to have appropriated the latter's theory to his own ends. Ibn Khaldun makes *asabiyyah* (lit. "clanism") the driving force of history. Not easily translated, the word denotes extremely strong group cohesion and morale. Its ultimate expression is *dulce et decorum est pro patria mori*. See Ibn Khaldun, *The Muqaddimah*, trans. Franz Rosenthal, abridged and ed. N. J. Dawood (Princeton, NJ: Princeton University Press, 2004), xi–xii, for an extended definition. For both Glubb and Ibn Khaldun, when *asabiyyah* is high, a civilization arises and flourishes; when lost, it dies. See Peter Turchin, *War and Peace and War* (New York, NY: Plume, 2007), for a contemporary theory of history inspired by Ibn Khaldun.

[4] For a description of wealth's catastrophic effect on Roman mores, see Sallust, *The Jugurthine War / The Conspiracy of Cataline*, trans. S. A. Handford (New York, NY: Penguin, 1964), 180–183.

[5] Edward Gibbon, *The History of the Decline and Fall of the Roman Empire*, ed. and abridged David P. Womersley (New York, NY: Penguin, 2001), 64.

[6] In *Day of Empire* (New York, NY: Anchor, 2009) Amy Chua argues that growing multicultural tolerance and openness dissolves the social

"glue" that makes empires cohere and thereby vitiates the élan that makes them great. See also the reference to Ibn Khaldun's *asabiyyah* in note 3 above.

[7] For graphic descriptions of what life is like when feral frivolity becomes the norm, see Theodore Dalrymple, *Life at the Bottom* (Chicago, IL: Ivan R. Dee, 2001).

[8] When a civilization no longer inspires its citizens and stops working for ordinary people, the formation of an "internal proletariat" divorced from the society's ideals, values, and goals becomes inevitable. See Arnold J. Toynbee, *A Study of History*, Vol. 1: Abridgement of Volumes I–VI by D. C. Somervell (New York, NY: Oxford University Press, 1987), passim. Even within the elite, those who lose out in the increasingly fierce competition for wealth, power, and status are "radicalized" and turn against the "system." See Turchin, op. cit., 277–281.

[9] Will and Ariel Durant, *The Lessons of History* (New York, NY: Simon & Schuster, 1968), 92.

[10] See William Ophuls, *Plato's Revenge* (Cambridge, MA: MIT Press, 2011), 70, 73, 78–80, 86–93, 102–105, 169–170, 174–177, for the numerous ways that civilizations necessarily frustrate the archetypal needs of human beings even under the best of circumstances. When a civilization begins to break down, frustration intensifies and spreads even to the privileged elite.

[11] See William Ophuls, *Requiem for Modern Politics* (Boulder, CO: Westview Press, 1997), 45–54.

[12] Edmund Burke, *Reflections on the Revolution in France*, ed. L. G. Mitchell (New York, NY: Oxford University Press, 2009), 141.

[13] For a fuller description of the emotional and cognitive shortcomings of human beings, see Ophuls, *Plato's Revenge*, 70–81.

Chapter 6

[1] Will Durant, *Our Oriental Heritage: The Story of Civilization*, vol. 1 (New York, NY: MJF Books, 1963), 4.

[2] See Mancur Olson, *The Rise and Decline of Nations* (New Haven, CT: Yale University Press, 1982). See also Carroll Quigley, *The Evolution of Civilizations*, 2nd ed. (Indianapolis, IN: Liberty Fund, 2010), 101–116, 416, on the perverse effects of "the institutionalization of social instruments."

[3] Barbara W. Tuchman, *A Distant Mirror* (New York, NY: Ballantine, 1987), 397. See also Arnold J. Toynbee, *A Study of History*, Vol. I: Abridgement of Vols. I–VI by D. C. Somervell (New York, NY: Oxford University Press, 1987), 555, on the "tendency toward standardization and uniformity" that overtakes a mature civilization.

[4] Ronald Wright, *A Short History of Progress* (New York, NY: Carroll & Graf, 2005), 109.

[5] William Playfair, *An Inquiry into the Permanent Causes of the Decline and Fall of the Powerful and Wealthy Nations* (Teddington, England: Wildhern Press, 2007), 28. See also Toynbee, op. cit., 307–352, on how societies cling to what has made them successful in the past and thereby fail to adapt to present circumstances. On the theme of success causing failure, see also Ian Morris, *Why the West Rules—For Now* (New York, NY: Farrar, Straus and Giroux, 2010).

[6] Tuchman, op. cit., 459. See also Cullen Murphy, *Are We Rome?* (Boston, MA: Mariner, 2007), 201.

[7] For a definitive account of how governments persist in acting contrary to their own interest despite the availability of feasible alternatives, see Barbara W. Tuchman, *The March of Folly* (New York, NY: Ballantine, 1985). Anthropologists have long noted that the initial response of primal peoples to radically changed circumstances is not adaptation, but a "revitalization movement"—that is, a fanatical, last-ditch, and often self-destructive effort to preserve the old ways—and the more successful the culture has been in the past, the more likely it is to resist change. See Anthony F. C. Wallace, "Revitalization Movements," *American Anthropologist* 58, no. 2 (1956): 264–281, and

Weston La Barre, *The Ghost Dance*, 3rd ed. (New York, NY: Delta, 1972). Even advanced civilizations fall into the same trap: see Wright, op. cit. 79, 102. See also Murphy, op. cit., 43–44, 47, on the "*omphalos* syndrome," the name given to the fatal tendency of successful empires to think that the world revolves around their navel and that they can simply impose their will on reality.

8   Thomas S. Kuhn, *The Structure of Scientific Revolutions*, 2nd ed. (Chicago, IL: Phoenix, 1970). See also Donella H. Meadows, *Thinking in Systems*, ed. Diana Wright (White River Junction, VT: Chelsea Green, 2008), 162–165, on the deep cultural resistance to shifts in the social paradigm.

9   Kuhn, op. cit., 76. See also Arthur Koestler, *The Sleepwalkers* (New York, NY: Penguin, 1990), 530.

10 See Peter Turchin, *War and Peace and War* (New York, NY: Plume, 2007), 257–259, 277–278, 281. See also David Hackett Fischer, *The Great Wave* (New York, NY: Oxford, 1996), 246–251.

11 When the elites defect, revolution impends. See Jack A. Goldstone, *Revolution and Rebellion in the Early Modern World* (Berkeley, CA: University of California Press, 1991), xxiii–xxiv, 9.

12 Technically, inflation is an expansion of the money supply relative to the goods available, but loose credit has the same effect. It expands the availability of money beyond what ecological and physical reality would otherwise support.

13 John Maynard Keynes, *The Economic Consequences of the Peace* (New York, NY: Skyhorse Publishing, 2007 [1919]), 134, emphasis in original.

14 Ibid.

15 One usually overlooked, but critically important, effect of inflation is that it exacerbates the disconnect between the real economy of nature and the artificial economy of money. Thus it has the effect of hastening ecological exhaustion. More generally, because it muddies the link between real and nominal values, inflation (along with loose

credit) creates a "money illusion," making it hard to know the true value of anything and encouraging reckless behavior. For an outstanding account of financial folly, see Carmen M. Reinhart and Kenneth Rogoff, *This Time Is Different* (Princeton, NJ: Princeton University Press, 2009). For inflation in particular, see Don Paarlberg, *An Analysis and History of Inflation* (Westport, CT: Praeger, 1992). For a classic description of one extraordinary episode, see Andrew Dickson White, *Fiat Money Inflation in France* (Seattle, WA: CreateSpace 2010 [1912]). Adam Fergusson, *When Money Dies* (New York, NY: Public Affairs, 2010) chronicles hyperinflation in Germany, Austria, and Hungary during the 1920s.

[16] See Hannah Arendt, *Crises of the Republic* (New York, NY: Harvest, 1972), 69.

[17] Otto Friedrich, *Before the Deluge* (New York, NY: Harper Perennial, 1995), 126. See also White, op. cit., 33, 58–59.

[18] According to Fischer, op. cit., 253, inflation is always a symptom of social imbalance, instability, and inequity, a kind of fever of the body economic with serious political consequences.

[19] Joseph A Tainter, "Complexity, Problem Solving, and Sustainable Societies," in Robert Costanza et al., eds. *Getting Down to Earth* (Washington, DC: Island Press, 1996), 61–76.

[20] Joseph A. Tainter, "Problem Solving: Complexity, History, Sustainability," *Population and Environment* 22, no.1 (September 2000), 23.

[21] Homer-Dixon, op. cit., 249.

[22] There are, of course, minor cycles of reform and revival within the larger historical cycle. Just as stocks do not go straight up or down, but oscillate within an overall trend, a civilization has its bull and bear moments, its little setbacks and resurgences, along the greater arc from conquest to decadence.

[23] Homer-Dixon, op. cit., 289.

[24] Niccolò Machiavelli, *The Prince and the Discourses*, trans. Luigi Ricci, rev. E. R. P. Vincent (New York: NY: McGraw-Hill, 1950), 21.

Conclusion

[1] William Playfair, *An Inquiry into the Permanent Causes of the Decline and Fall of Powerful and Wealthy Nations* (Teddington, England: Wildhern Press, 2007 [1807]), 58.

[2] Edward Gibbon, *The History of the Decline and Fall of the Roman Empire*, ed. and abridged David P. Womersley (New York, NY: Penguin, 2001), 435.

[3] Playfair, op cit., 204.

[4] This book is about the process of decline and fall in general, not about the destiny of any particular society. Nevertheless, a brief word about the fate of the American empire may be apropos. Despite its current difficulties, the United States retains many geopolitical advantages and has enormous potential to thrive in an increasingly networked world. See Anne-Marie Slaughter, "America's Edge," *Foreign Affairs*, March/April 2009, 94-113, for what this will take, and Jean-Marie Guéhenno, *The End of the Nation-State*, trans. Victoria Elliott (Minneapolis, MN: University of Minnesota Press, 1995), for a provocative vision of a networked future. However, whether the world can remain networked even to its current extent once critical shortages of energy and materials emerge in the decades to come remains an open question. For an argument that it cannot—that, in fact, radical relocalization impends—see Jeff Rubin, *Why Your World Is About to Get a Whole Lot Smaller* (New York, NY: Random House, 2009). It is also an open question whether the United States can desist from suicidal stupidity. Despite rising criticism at home and abroad, it persists in simultaneously pursuing all three major pathways to self-destruction mentioned in the previous chapter: war, debt, and inflation. This cannot have a happy ending. To learn more, see Simon Schama, *Citizens* (New York, NY: Vintage, 1990) on how a quagmire of debt precipitated a

revolution; Paul Kennedy, *The Rise and Fall of the Great Powers* (New York, NY: Vintage, 1989) for how imperial overstretch leads to ruin; and Jack A. Goldstone, *Revolution and Rebellion in the Early Modern World* (Berkeley, CA: University of California Press, 1991), for how selfish and short-sighted elites either fail to act or act in ways that make matters worse. (See especially Goldstone's concluding remarks on the decline of the United States, 485–497.)

[5] See Immanuel Wallerstein, "The Global Economy Won't Recover, Now or Ever," *Foreign Policy*, January/February 2011, 76, for a succinct and trenchant summary of why "the historical system in which we are living is in structural crisis and will not survive." Some would argue that China, India, and the other so-called emerging economies are exempt from the crisis, but their emergence is predicated on the (continuing) operation of that historical system. In the end, they seem destined to enact the same tragedy as the so-called developed economies, but at a faster pace. For instance, despite being at a much earlier stage in its economic development, China's ecological predicament is in many respects far worse than that of the United States.

[6] I use James Watt's steam engine (1763–75) as the beginning of the industrial era.

[7] Joseph A. Tainter, *The Collapse of Complex Societies* (Cambridge, England: Cambridge University Press, 1988), 214.

[8] Tainter, op. cit., 209.

[9] Ronald Wright, *A Short History of Progress* (New York, NY: Carroll & Graf, 2005), 34. For example, except among a few rural relicts, chicken coops and vegetable gardens are a distant memory; everyone else depends completely on supermarkets. Thus the survival skills that saw many through the Great Depression in the US, or the aftermath of World War II in Japan, are virtually extinct.

[10] Nevertheless, as it has in the past, relative backwardness may confer important advantages during the breakdown of the current civilization. See Ian Morris, *Why The West Rules—For Now* (New York, NY:

Farrar, Straus and Giroux, 2010), 34, 179, 195, 331–334, 564, for a discussion of this particular "paradox of development."

11. Tainter, op. cit., 214.

12. James Lovelock, "A Book for All Seasons," *Science* 280, no. 5365 (May 8, 1998): 832–833, urges the preparation of a "Bible" incorporating all the scientific knowledge required to restart a complex civilization after an extended dark age. However, John Michael Greer, *The Long Descent* (Gabriola Island, BC: New Society, 2008), 182–187, believes that Lovelock's approach would foster scholasticism rather than science, that posterity would turn such a "Bible" into a beautiful but useless illuminated manuscript. He argues that we must instead preserve the methods and mindset of science, not the accumulated knowledge itself, for with these fundamentals the knowledge can always be recreated. Greer's *The Ecotechnic Future* (Gabriola Island, BC: New Society, 2009) contains specific proposals toward this end.

13. Joseph A. Tainter, "Complexity, Problem Solving, and Sustainable Societies," in Robert Costanza et al., eds. *Getting Down to Earth* (Washington, DC: Island Press, 1996), 61–76, n 4.

14. The stages that individuals go through when faced with terminal illness—from early denial to ultimate accommodation—can illuminate the struggle of a society confronted with an unwelcome and painful loss of wealth and power. See Elisabeth Kübler-Ross, *On Death and Dying* (New York, NY: Scribner, 1997).

15. Such is the argument of my *Plato's Revenge* (Cambridge, MA: MIT Press, 2011), 129–193.

Selected Sources

Ahmed, Nafeez Mosaddeq. *A User's Guide to the Crisis of Civilization*. New York, NY: Pluto Press, 2010.

Arendt, Hannah. *Crises of the Republic*. New York, NY: Harvest, 1972.

Bak, Per. *How NatureWorks*. New York, NY: Springer, 1999.

Bartlett, Albert A., et al. *The Essential Exponential*. Lincoln, NE: University of Nebraska Center for Science, Mathematics & Computer Education, 2004.

Barzun, Jacques. *From Dawn to Decadence*. New York, NY: Harper Perennial, 2001.

Bettelheim, Bruno. *Freud and Man's Soul*. New York, NY: Vintage, 1984.

Brander, B. G. *Staring Into Chaos*. Dallas, TX: Spence, 1998.

Brander, James A. "Presidential Address: Innovation in retrospect and prospect." *Canadian Journal of Economics* 43, no. 4 (November 2010): 1087–1121.

Braudel, Fernand. *The Mediterranean and the MediterraneanWorld in the Age of Philip II*, vols. 1 and 2. Berkeley, CA: University of California Press, 1996.

Brown, Harrison. *The Challenge of Man's Future*. New York, NY: Viking, 1954.

Burke, Edmund. *Reflections on the Revolution in France*, edited L. G. Mitchell. New York, NY: Oxford, 2009.

Campbell, Colin J., and Jean H. Laherrère. "The End of Cheap Oil." *Scientific American* (March 1998): 80–85.

Carter, Vernon Gill, and Tom Dale. *Topsoil and Civilization*. Norman, OK: University of Oklahoma Press, 1975.

Catton, William R. *Overshoot*. Champaign, IL: Illini Books, 1982.

Chua, Amy. *Day of Empire*. New York, NY: Anchor, 2009.

Clastres, Pierre. *Society Against the State*. New York, NY: Urizen, 1977.

Cohen, Mark Nathan. *The Food Crisis in Prehistory*. New Haven, CT: Yale University Press, 1977.

Cohen, Mark Nathan. *Health and the Rise of Civilization*. New Haven, CT: Yale University Press, 1991.

Connor, W. R. "Why Were We Surprised?" *American Scholar* 60, no. 2 (Spring 1991): 175–184.

Cottrell, Fred. *Energy and Society*. New York, NY: McGraw-Hill, 1955.

Cowen, Tyler. *The Great Stagnation*. Seattle, WA: Amazon Kindle, 2011.

Crone, Patricia. *Pre-Industrial Societies*. Oxford, England: Oneworld, 2003.

Dalrymple, Theodore. *Life at the Bottom*. Chicago, IL: Ivan R. Dee, 2001.

Daly, Herman E. *Beyond Growth*. Boston, MA: Beacon Press, 1997.

Darwin, Charles Galton. *The Next Million Years*. New York, NY: Doubleday, 1953.

Diamond, Jared. *Collapse*. New York, NY: Penguin, 2006.

Diamond, Jared. *Guns, Germs, and Steel*. New York, NY: W. W. Norton, 2005.

Diamond, Jared. "The Worst Mistake in the History of the Human Race." *Discover* (May 1987): 64–66.

Durant, Will and Ariel. *The Lessons of History*. New York, NY: Simon & Schuster, 1968.

Ferguson, Niall. "Complexity and Collapse." *Foreign Affairs* 89 no. 2 (March/April 2010): 18–32.

Fergusson, Adam. *When Money Dies*. New York, NY: Public Affairs, 2010.

Ferrero, Guglielmo. *Characters and Events of Roman History*. New York, NY: Barnes and Noble, 2005.

Fischer, David Hackett. *The Great Wave*. New York, NY: Oxford University Press, 1996.

Fox, Robin. *The Search for Society*. New Brunswick, NJ: Rutgers University Press, 1989.

Freud, Sigmund. *Civilization and Its Discontents*, translated by James Strachey. New York, NY: Norton, 1961.

Georgescu-Roegen, Nicholas. *The Entropy Law and the Economic Process*. Cambridge, MA: Harvard University Press, 1971.

Georgescu-Roegen, Nicholas. "Energy and Economic Myths," *Southern Economic Journal* 41, no. 3 (January 1975): 347–381.

Gibbon, Edward. *The History of the Decline and Fall of the Roman Empire*, edited and abridged by David P. Womersley. New York, NY: Penguin, 2001.

Glubb, Sir John. *The Fate of Empires and Search for Survival*. Edinburgh, Scotland: William Blackwood, 1978.

Goldstone, Jack A. *Revolution and Rebellion in the Early Modern World*. Berkeley, CA: University of California Press, 1991.

Grant, Michael. *The Fall of the Roman Empire—A Reappraisal*. New York, NY: Crown, 1982.

Greer, John Michael. *The Ecotechnic Future*. Gabriola Island, BC: New Society, 2009.

Greer, John Michael. *The Long Descent*. Gabriola Island, BC: New Society, 2008.

Greer, John Michael. *The Wealth of Nature*. Gabriola Island, BC: New Society, 2011.

Gribbin, John. *Deep Simplicity*. New York, NY: Random House, 2004.

Guéhenno, Jean-Marie. *The End of the Nation-State*, translated by Victoria Elliott. Minneapolis, MN: University of Minnesota Press, 1995.

Hall, Charles A. S., et al. "Peak Oil, EROI, Investments and the Economy in an Uncertain Future" in *Biofuels, Solar and Wind as Renewable Energy Systems*, edited David Pimentel. New York, NY: Springer, 2008, 109–132.

Hall, Charles A. S., et al. "What Is the Minimum EROI That a Sustainable Society Must Have?" *Energies* 2, no. 1 (2009): 25–47.

Hall, Charles A. S., and John W. Day, Jr. "Revisiting the Limits to Growth After Peak Oil." *American Scientist* 97 (May–June 2009): 230–237.

Hanson, Victor Davis. *Fields Without Dreams*. New York, NY: Free Press, 1997.

Hayek, F. A. *The Road to Serfdom*, edited by Bruce Caldwell. Chicago, IL: University of Chicago Press, 2007.

Heather, Peter. *The Fall of the Roman Empire*. New York, NY: Oxford University Press, 2007.

Heinrich, Bernd. "Clear-Cutting the Truth About Trees." *The New York Times* (December 20, 2009).

Hesiod. *Theogony and Works and Days*, translated by M. L. West. New York, NY: Oxford University Press, 2009.

Homer-Dixon, Thomas. *The Ingenuity Gap*. New York, NY: Vintage, 2002.

Homer-Dixon, Thomas. *The Upside of Down*. Washington, DC: Island Press, 2006.

Hughes, J. Donald. *Pan's Travail*. Baltimore, MD: Johns Hopkins University Press, 1996.

Ibn Khaldun. *The Muqaddimah*, translated by Franz Rosenthal, abridged and edited by N. J. Dawood. Princeton, NJ: Princeton University Press, 1967.

Illich, Ivan. *Energy and Equity*. London, England: Calder and Boyars, 1974.

Jacobs, Jane. *Cities and the Wealth of Nations*. New York, NY: Random House, 1984.

Jacobs, Jane. *Dark Age Ahead*. New York, NY: Vintage, 2005.

Kahn, Herman, and Anthony J. Wiener. *The Year 2000*. New York, NY: Macmillan, 1967.

Kennedy, Paul. *The Rise and Fall of the Great Powers*. New York, NY: Vintage, 1989.

Keynes, John Maynard. *The Economic Consequences of the Peace*. New York, NY: Skyhorse, 2007.

Kindleberger, Charles P., et al. *Manias, Panics, and Crashes*, 5th edition. New York, NY: Wiley, 2005.

King, F. H. *Farmers of Forty Centuries*. Mineola, NY: Dover, 2004.

Koestler, Arthur. *The Sleepwalkers*. New York, NY: Penguin, 1990.

Kohr, Leopold. *The Breakdown of Nations*. New York, NY: Dutton, 1978.

Kohr, Leopold. *The Overdeveloped Nations*. New York, NY: Dutton, 1978.

Kuhn, Thomas S. *The Structure of Scientific Revolutions*, 2nd edition. Chicago, IL: Phoenix, 1970.

La Barre, Weston. *The Ghost Dance*, 3rd edition. New York, NY: Delta, 1972.

Le Bon, Gustave. *The Crowd*. Mineola, NY: Dover, 2002.

Lévi-Strauss, Claude. *Tristes Tropiques*, translated by John and Doreen Weightman. New York, NY: Atheneum, 1974.

Lovelock, James. "A Book for All Seasons." *Science* 280, no. 5365 (May 8, 1998): 832–833.

Mackenzie, Debora. "Why the Demise of Civilisation May Be Inevitable." *New Scientist* 2650 (April 5, 2008): 32–35.

Mackenzie, Debora. "Will a Pandemic Bring Down Civilisation?" *New Scientist* 2650 (April 5, 2008): 28–31.

Márquez, Gabriel García. *One Hundred Years of Solitude*. New York, NY: Harper Perennial, 2006.

Marsh, George Perkins. *Man and Nature*. New York, NY: General Books, 2009 [1864].

McNeill, William H. *Polyethnicity and National Unity in World History*. Toronto, Ontario: University of Toronto Press, 1986.

Meadows, Donella H. "Systems Dynamics Meets the Press." *In Context* (Autumn 1989), 16–21.

Meadows, Donella H. *Thinking in Systems*, edited by Diana Wright. White River Junction, VT: Chelsea Green, 2008.

Meadows, Donella, Jorgen Randers, and Dennis Meadows. *Limits to Growth: The 30-Year Update*. White River Junction, VT: Chelsea Green, 2004.

Mitchell, Melanie. *Complexity*. New York, NY: Oxford, 2009.

Miller, John H., and Scott E. Page. *Complex Adaptive Systems*. Princeton, NJ: Princeton University Press, 2007.

Montesquieu, Charles de Secondat, baron de. *Considerations on the Causes of the Greatness of the Romans and their Decline*, translated by David Lowenthal. Indianapolis, IN: Hackett, 1999.

Montgomery, David R. *Dirt*. Berkeley, CA: University of California Press, 2008.

Morris, Ian. *Why the West Rules—For Now*. New York, NY: Farrar, Straus and Giroux, 2010.

Motyl, Alexander J. *Imperial Ends*. New York, NY: Columbia University Press, 2001.

Murphy, Cullen. *Are We Rome?* Boston, MA: Mariner, 2007.

Neruda, Pablo. *The Heights of Macchu Picchu*, bilingual edition, translated by Nathaniel Tarn. New York, NY: Farrar, Straus and Giroux, 1966.

Olson, Mancur. *The Rise and Decline of Nations*. New Haven, CT: Yale, 1982.

Ophuls, William. *Ecology and the Politics of Scarcity*. San Francisco, CA: W. H. Freeman, 1977.

Ophuls, William. *Plato's Revenge*. Cambridge, MA: MIT Press, 2011.

Ophuls, William. *Requiem for Modern Politics*. Boulder, CO: Westview, 1997.

Ormerod, Paul. *Why Most Things Fail*. New York, NY: Wiley, 2007.

Paarlberg, Don. *An Analysis and History of Inflation*. Westport, CT: Praeger, 1992.

Page, Scott E. *Understanding Complexity*. Chantilly, VA: The Teaching Company, 2009.

Parkinson, C. Northcote. *Parkinson's Law*. New York, NY: Ballantine 1987.

Pimentel, David, and Marcia H. Pimentel. *Food, Energy, and Society*, 3rd edition. Boca Raton, FL: CRC Press, 2007.

Plato. *The Republic of Plato*, translated by Allan Bloom. New York, NY: Basic Books, 1968.

Playfair, William. *An Inquiry into the Permanent Causes of the Decline and Fall of the Powerful and Wealthy Nations*. Teddington, England: Wildhern Press, 2007.

Polanyi, Karl. *The Great Transformation*. Boston, MA: Beacon, 1957.

Polybius. *The Histories*, translated by Robin Waterfield. New York, NY: Oxford, 2010.

Ponting, Clive. *A Green History of the World*, revised and updated. New York, NY: Penguin, 2007.

Quigley, Carroll. *The Evolution of Civilizations*, 2nd edition. Indianapolis, IN: Liberty Fund, 2010.

Quinn, Daniel. *Ishmael*. New York, NY: Bantam, 1992.

Quinn, Daniel. *The Story of B*. New York, NY: Bantam, 1997.

Reinhart, Carmen M., and Kenneth Rogoff. *This Time Is Different*. Princeton, NJ: Princeton University Press, 2009

Rifkin, Jeremy. *Entropy*. New York, NY: Bantam, 1981.

Rousseau, Jean-Jacques. *The First and Second Discourses*, edited by Roger D. Masters and translated by Judith R. Masters. New York, NY: St. Martin's, 1964.

Rubin, Jeff. *Why Your World Is About to Get a Whole Lot Smaller*. New York, NY: Random House, 2009.

Ruddiman, William F. *Plows, Plagues, and Petroleum*. Princeton, NJ: Princeton University Press, 2007.

Ryan, Charles J. "The Choices in the Next Energy and Social Revolution." *Technological Forecasting and Social Change* 16, no. 3 (1980): 191–208.

Ryan, Charles J. "The Overdeveloped Society." *Stanford Magazine* (Fall/Winter 1979): 58–65.

Sallust. *The Jugurthine War / The Conspiracy of Cataline*, translated by S. A. Handford. New York, NY: Penguin, 1964.

Schama, Simon. *Citizens*. New York, NY: Vintage, 1990.

Slaughter, Anne-Marie. "America's Edge." *Foreign Affairs* (March/April 2009): 94–113.

Smil, Vaclav. *Why America Is Not a New Rome*. Cambridge, MA: MIT Press, 2010.

Solomon, Steven. *Water*. New York, NY: Harper, 2010.

Sorokin, Pitirim A. *The Crisis of Our Age*. New York, NY: Dutton, 1944.

Sorokin, Pitirim A. *Social and Cultural Dynamics*, revised and abridged. Boston, MA: Porter Sargent, 1957.

Spengler, Oswald. *The Decline of the West*, abridged. New York, NY: Vintage, 2006.

Tainter, Joseph A. *The Collapse of Complex Societies*. Cambridge, England: Cambridge University Press, 1988.

Tainter, Joseph A. "Complexity, Problem Solving, and Sustainable Societies" in Robert Costanza et al., eds. *Getting Down to Earth*. Washington, DC: Island Press, 1996, 61–76.

Tainter, Joseph A. "Human Resource Use: Timing and Implications for Sustainability." Paper delivered to 94th Annual Meeting of the Ecological Society of America (2009), archived at http://www.oildrum.com/node/6942.

Tainter, Joseph A. "Problem Solving: Complexity, History, Sustainability." *Population and Environment* 22, no. 1 (September 2000): 3–41.

Taleb, Nassim Nicholas. *The Black Swan*, 2nd edition. New York, NY: Random House, 2010.

Thiel, Peter. "The End of the Future." *National Review* (October 3, 2011).

Thoreau, Henry David. *Walden and Other Writings*, edited by Joseph Wood Krutch. New York, NY: Bantam, 1962.

Toynbee, Arnold J. *Mankind and Mother Earth*. New York, NY: Oxford University Press, 1976.

Toynbee, Arnold J. *A Study of History*, Vol. 1: Abridgement of Volumes I–VI by D. C. Somervell. New York, NY: Oxford University Press, 1987.

Tuchman, Barbara W. *A Distant Mirror*. New York, NY: Ballantine, 1987.

Tuchman, Barbara W. *The March of Folly*. New York, NY: Ballantine, 1985.

Tudge, Colin. Neanderthals, Bandits and Farmers. New Haven, CT: Yale University Press, 1999.

Turchin, Peter. *War and Peace and War*. New York, NY: Plume, 2007.

Vico, Giambattista. *New Science*, 3rd edition, translated by David Marsh. New York, NY: Penguin, 2000.

Wackernagel, Mathis, and William Rees. *Our Ecological Footprint*. Gabriola Island, BC: New Society, 1996.

Wallace, Anthony F. C. "Revitalization Movements." *American Anthropologist* 52, no. 2 (1956): 264–281.

Wallerstein, Emmanuel. "The Global Economy Won't Recover, Now or Ever." *Foreign Policy* (January/February 2011): 76.

Ward-Perkins, Bryan. *The Fall of Rome and the End of Civilization*. New York, NY: Oxford University Press, 2006.

White, Andrew Dickson. *Fiat Money Inflation in France*. Seattle, WA: CreateSpace, 2010.

Wright, Ronald. *A Short History of Progress*. New York, NY: Carroll & Graf, 2005.

Index

Adams, John 45, 56
Agriculture 7–8, 10–11, 22–23, 67
Ataturk, Mustafa Kemal 63-64
Bak, Per 37
Bartlett, Albert 13
Berry, Wendell ii
Burke, Edmund 53
Byzantine Empire i, 3
Chateaubriand, François-René de 7
Complexity 31-43, 55–56, 59
    and bureaucracy 35–36
    and chaos 36–40
    and energy 35
Cowen, Tyler 34
Durant, Ariel 3, 50, 71
Durant, Will 3, 4, 39–40, 50, 55, 71
Ecology 7–12
    and carrying capacity 11, 19
    and law of the minimum 10–11
    and limits 9–10, 12
    and market failure 11–12
Eddington, Arthur Stanley 21
Entropy 21–29. *See also* Moral entropy, Ther-modynamics
    and electrical power 24–25
    and EROI (EROEI) 27-29
    and net energy 27–29
    as hidden cost of technology 25–28
    as loss of usefulness 21–24
    as tax 28
EROI (EROEI). *See* Entropy
Exponential growth 13–19, 62
    defined 13
    and technology 17–19
Ferguson, Niall 40
Fischer, David Hackett 73
Freud, Sigmund 74
Friedrich, Otto 61
Gibbon, Edward front, 2, 3, 48, 65, 66
Glubb, John Bagot (Glubb Pasha) 46-50, 51, 52, 66, 67, 86n2, n3
Goldstone, Jack A. 73
Greer, John Michael 72
Gribbin, John 74
Hayek, F. A. 74
Homer-Dixon, Thomas 33, 39, 63, 64, 72
Hubris 2, 47, 62, 66, 68, 69
Ibn Khaldun 45, 86n3

Inflation 15, 18, 59-62
Kahn, Herman 1, 19
Keynes, John Maynard 60-62
Kuhn, Thomas S. 58
Le Bon, Gustave 45, 74
Lévi-Strauss, Claude 74
Livy 3–4
Machiavelli, Niccolò 1, 3, 64
Márquez, Gabriel García 75
Meadows, Donella H. 31, 37, 38, 73–74
Meiji Reformation 63–64
Miller, John H. 74
Mitchell, Melanie 74
Moral entropy 51-53
  and inflation 61
Morality 45-53
Morris, Ian 71-72
Neolithic Revolution 7
Neruda, Pablo 3, 75
Net energy. *See* Entropy
Ormerod, Paul 31
Ottoman Empire i, 3, 63–64
Overshoot and collapse 11–12

Page, Scott E. 37, 74
Parkinson, C. Northcote 35
Playfair, William 57, 65-66
Prudence 41, 56, 61, 68–69
Psychology, human
  as holdover from Paleolithic 17–18, 31
  and instrumental rationality 18
Quinn, Daniel 75
Rome 4, 8, 28, 34, 35, 48
Schama, Simon 74
Seneca 7
Spengler, Oswald 46, 50, 51
Tainter, Joseph A. 32-34, 63, 66–67, 68, 73
Taleb, Nassim Nicholas 74
Thermodynamics. *See also* Entropy
  and automobile 25
  and embodied energy 25
  laws of 21-22
Tuchman, Barbara 56-57
Water 8, 10–11
Wisdom. *See* Prudence
Wright, Ronald 57, 67, 75

Printed in Great Britain
by Amazon